D0520717

SUPER COOKERY

Quick & Easy

p

This is a Parragon Publishing Book
This edition published in 2001

Parragon Publishing
Queen Street House
4 Queen Street
Bath BA1 1HE, UK

ISBN: 0-75255-274-0

Printed in China

Note
Cup measurements used in this book are for American cups.
Tablespoons are assumed to be 15 ml. Unless otherwise stated,
milk is assumed to be full fat, eggs are medium and pepper is
freshly ground black pepper.

Contents

Introduction   4

Soups & Starters   8

Salads & Snacks   112

Meat & Poultry   200

Fish & Seafood   330

Desserts & Puddings   440

Index   510

Introduction

This book is designed to appeal to anyone who wants a wholesome but quick and easy diet, and includes many recipes suitable for vegetarians and vegans. Its main aim is to show people that, with a little forethought, it is possible to spend very little time in the kitchen while still enjoying appetizing food.

The recipes collected together come from all over the world; some of the Indian and barbeque dishes featured require marinating, often overnight, but it is worth remembering that their actual cooking time is very short once the marinade has been absorbed. The more exotic dishes on offer are balanced by some traditional dishes which are sure to be firm family favorites. If you want fast food for everyday meals, or you are short on time and want to prepare a tasty dinner party treat, there is something for everybody in this book.

To save time in the kitchen, always make sure that you have the requisite basics in your cupboard. By keeping a stock of staple foodstuffs such as rice, pasta, spices, and herbs, you can easily turn your hand to any number of these recipes.

KEEPING A FULL STORE-CUPBOARD

Flour

You will need to keep a selection of flour: Self-raising and Wholewheat are the most useful. You may also like to keep some rice flour and cornstarch for thickening sauces and to add to cakes, cookies, and puddings. Buckwheat, garbanzo bean, and soya flours can also be bought. These are useful for combining with other flours to add different flavors and textures.

Grains and Rice

A good variety of grains is essential. For rice, choose from long-grain, basmati, Italian arborio, short-grain, and wild rice. Look out for fragrant Thai rice, jasmine rice, and combinations of different varieties to add color and texture to your dishes. When choosing your rice, remember that brown rice is a better source of vitamin B1 and fiber.

Other grains add variety to the diet. Try to include some barley millet, bulghur wheat, polenta, oats, semolina, sago, and tapioca.

Pasta

Pasta is very popular nowadays, and there are many types and shapes to choose from. Keep a good selection, such as basic lasagne sheets, tagliatelle, or fettuccine (flat ribbons), and spaghetti. For a change, sample some of the many fresh pastas now available. Better still, make your own—handrolling pasta can be very satisfying, and you can buy a special machine for rolling the dough and cutting certain shapes.

Dried Legumes

Legumes are a valuable source of protein, vitamins, and minerals. Stock up on soya beans, navy beans, red kidney beans, cannellini beans, garbanzo beans, lentils, split peas, and butter beans. Buy dried legumes for soaking and cooking yourself, or canned varieties for speed and convenience.

Herbs

A good selection of herbs is important for adding variety to your cooking. Fresh herbs are preferable to dried, but it is essential to have dried ones in stock as a useful back-up. You should store dried basil, thyme, bay leaves, oregano, rosemary, mixed herbs, and bouquet garni.

Chiles

These come both fresh and dried and in many colors. The "hotness" varies, so use with caution. The seeds are hottest and are usually discarded. Chili powder should also be used sparingly. Check whether the powder is pure chili or a chili seasoning or blend, which should be milder.

Nuts and Seeds

As well as adding protein, vitamins, and useful fats to the diet, nuts and seeds add important flavor and texture to vegetarian meals. Make sure that you keep a good supply of nuts such as hazelnuts, pine nuts, and walnuts. Coconut is useful too.

For your seed collection, have sesame, sunflower, pumpkin, and poppy. Pumpkin seeds in particular are a good source of zinc.

Dried Fruits

Currants, raisins, golden raisins, dates, apples, apricots, figs, pears, peaches, prunes, papayas, mangoes, figs, bananas, and pineapples can all be purchased dried and can be used in lots of different recipes. When buying dried fruits, look for untreated varieties: for example, buy figs that have not been rolled in sugar, and choose unsulfured apricots, if they are available.

Oils and Fats

Oils are useful for adding subtle flavorings to foods, so it is a good idea to have a selection in your store-cupboard. Use a light olive oil for cooking and extra-virgin olive oil for salad dressings. Use sunflower oil as a good general-purpose oil. Sesame oil is wonderful in stir-fries; hazelnut and walnut oils are superb in salad dressings. Oils and fats add flavor to foods, and contain all the important fat-soluble vitamins A, D, E, and K. Remember all fats and oils are high in calories, and that oils are higher in calories than butter or margarine.

Vinegars

Choose three or four vinegars—red or white wine, cider, light malt, tarragon, sherry, or balsamic vinegar, to name just a few. Each will add its own character to your recipes.

Mustards

Mustards are made from black, brown, or white mustard seeds, which are ground and mixed with spices. Meaux mustard is made from mixed mustard seeds and has a grainy texture with a warm taste. Dijon mustard, made from husked and ground mustard seeds, has a sharp flavor. Its versatility in salads and with barbeques makes it ideal for the vegetarian. German mustard is mild and is best used in Scandinavian and German dishes.

Bottled Sauces

Soy sauce is widely used in Eastern cookery and is made from fermented yellow soya beans mixed with wheat, salt, yeast, and sugar. Light soy sauce tends to be rather salty, whereas dark soy sauce tends to be sweeter. Teriyaki sauce gives an authentic Japanese flavoring to stir-fries. Black bean and yellow bean sauces add an instant authentic Chinese flavor to stir-fries.

STORING SPICES

Your basic stock of spices should include fresh ginger and garlic, chili powder, turmeric, paprika, cloves, cardamom, black pepper, ground coriander, and ground cumin. The powdered spices will keep very well in airtight containers, while the fresh ginger and garlic will keep for 7-10 days in the refrigerator. Other useful items, to be acquired as your repertoire increases, are cumin seeds (black as well as white), onion seeds, mustard seeds, cloves, cinnamon, dried red chiles, fenugreek, vegetable ghee, and garam masala (a mixture of spices that can either be bought ready-made or home-made in quantity for use whenever required).

USING SPICES

You can use spices whole, ground, roasted, fried, or mixed with yogurt to marinate meat and poultry. One spice can alter the flavor of a dish and a combination of several can produce different colors and textures. The quantities of spices shown in the recipes are merely a guide. Increase or decrease them as you wish, especially in the cases of salt and chili powder, which are a matter of taste.

Many of the recipes in this book call for ground spices, which are generally available in supermarkets as well as in Indian and Pakistani grocers. In India whole spices are ground at home, and there is no doubt that freshly ground spices do make a noticeable difference to the taste.

Some recipes require roasted spices. In India, this is done on a *thawa*, but you can use a heavy, ideally cast-iron skillet. No water or oil is needed: the spices are simply dry-roasted whole while the pan is shaken to stop them burning on the bottom of the pan.

Remember that long cooking over a lowish heat will improve the taste of the food as it allows the spices to be absorbed. This is why re-heating dishes the following day is no problem for most Indian food.

USEFUL ORIENTAL INGREDIENTS
Bamboo Shoots
These are added for texture, as they have very little flavor. Available in cans, they are a common ingredient in Chinese cooking.

Beansprouts
These are mung bean shoots, which are very nutritious, containing many vitamins. They add crunch to a recipe and are widely available. Do not overcook them, as they wilt and do not add texture to the dish.

Black Beans
These are soy beans and are very salty. They can be bought, and crushed with salt, and then rinsed or used in the form of a ready-made sauce for convenience.

Chinese Beans

These long beans may be eaten whole and are very tender. Green beans may also be used.

Chinese Five-Spice Powder
An aromatic blend of cinnamon, cloves, star anise, fennel, and brown peppercorns. It is often used in marinades.

Chinese Leaves
A light green leaf with a sweet flavor. It can be found readily in most supermarkets.

Hoisin Sauce
A dark brown, sweet, thick sauce that is widely available. It is made from spices, soy sauce, garlic, and chili, and is often served as a dipping sauce.

Lychees

These are worth buying fresh, as they are easy to prepare. Inside the inedible skin is a fragrant white fruit. Lychees are available canned and are a classic ingredient.

Mango

Choose a ripe mango for its sweet, scented flesh. If a mango is underripe when bought, leave it in a sunny place for a few days before using.

Noodles

The Chinese use several varieties of noodle. You will probably find it easier to use the readily available dried varieties, such as egg noodles, which are yellow, rice stick noodles, which are white and very fine, or transparent noodles, which are opaque when dry, and turn transparent on cooking. However, cellophane or rice noodles may be used instead.

Oyster Sauce

Readily available, this sauce is made from oysters, salt, seasonings, and cornstarch, and is brown in color.

Pak Choi

Also known as Chinese cabbage, this has a mild, slightly bitter flavor.

Rice Vinegar

This has a mild, sweet taste that is quite delicate. It is available in some supermarkets, but if not available use cider vinegar instead.

Rice Wine

This is similar to dry sherry in color, alcohol content, and smell, but it is worth buying rice wine for its distinctive flavor.

Sesame Oil

This is made from roasted sesame seeds and has an intense flavor. It burns easily and is therefore added at the end of cooking for flavor, and is not used for frying.

Soy Sauce

This is widely available, but it is worth buying a good grade of sauce. It is produced in both light and dark varieties—the former is used with fish and vegetables for a lighter color and flavor, while the latter, being darker, richer, saltier, and more intense, is used as a dipping sauce or with strongly flavored meats.

Star Anise

This is an eight-pointed, star-shaped pod with a strong aniseed flavor. The spice is also available ground. If a pod is added to a dish, it should be removed before serving.

Szechwan Pepper

This is quite hot and spicy and should be used sparingly. It is bright red in color and is readily available in the shops.

Bean Curd

This soya bean paste is available in several forms. The cake variety, which is soft and spongy and a white-gray color, is used in this book. It is very bland, but adds texture to dishes, and is perfect for absorbing all the other flavors in the dish.

Water Chestnuts

These are flat and round and can usually only be purchased in cans, already peeled. They add a delicious crunch to dishes and have a sweet flavor.

Yellow Beans

Again a soy bean and very salty. Use a variety that is chunky rather than smooth.

Soups & Starters

The soups and starters in this chapter combine a variety of flavors and textures from all over the world. There are thicker soups, thin clear consommés, and soups to appeal to vegetarians. The range of soups include thick and creamy winter warmers and light and spicy Oriental recpies. Many have been chosen because of their nutritional content and may be eaten as part of a low-fat diet. All, however, can be eaten as starters or as a light snack. With the addition of other types of starters, you will find something to suit every taste—and all are delicious.

All of these recipes are easy to prepare and appetizing. They are colorful and flavorsome, providing an excellent beginning to any dinner party or just for an everyday snack. Depending on the main course, whet your guests' appetite with a tasty Dhal Soup, Prawn Omelet, or Oriental Thai Chicken Noodle Soup. All of these dishes are sure to get your meal off to the right start.

Thai Chicken Noodle Soup

Serves 4–6

INGREDIENTS

1 sheet of dried egg noodles from a 9 ounce pack	2 garlic cloves, chopped	3 tablespoons peanut butter
1 tablespoon oil	3/4-inch piece fresh ginger root, finely chopped	2 tablespoons light soy sauce
4 skinless, boneless chicken thighs, diced	3 3/4 cups chicken stock	1 small red bell pepper, chopped
1 bunch scallions, sliced	scant 1 cup coconut milk	1/2 cup frozen peas
	1 tablespoon red Thai curry paste	salt and pepper

1 Put the noodles in a shallow dish and soak in boiling water following the instructions on the packet.

2 Heat the oil in a large saucepan or wok, add the chicken, and fry for 5 minutes, stirring until lightly browned. Add the white part of the scallions, the garlic, and ginger and fry for 2 minutes, stirring constantly. Add the stock, coconut milk, curry paste, peanut butter, and soy sauce. Season with salt and pepper to taste. Bring to a boil, stirring constantly, then simmer for 8 minutes, stirring occasionally. Add the red bell pepper, peas, and green scallion tops and cook for 2 minutes.

3 Add the drained noodles and heat through. Spoon into individual bowls and serve with a spoon and fork.

VARIATION

Green Thai curry paste can be used for a less fiery flavor. It is available from specialty gourmet stores.

Chicken & Pasta Broth

Serves 6

INGREDIENTS

12 ounces boneless chicken breasts	1½ cups diced carrots	1 cup small pasta shapes
2 tablespoons sunflower oil	9 ounces cauliflower flowerets	salt and pepper
1 medium onion, diced	3¾ cups chicken stock	Parmesan cheese (optional)
	2 teaspoons dried mixed herbs	and crusty bread, to serve
---

1 Using a sharp knife, finely dice the chicken, discarding any skin.

2 Heat the oil in a large saucepan and quickly sauté the chicken and vegetables until they are lightly colored.

3 Stir in the stock and herbs. Bring to a boil and add the pasta. Return to a boil, cover, and simmer for 10 minutes, stirring occasionally to prevent the pasta shapes from sticking together.

4 Season with salt and pepper to taste and sprinkle with Parmesan cheese, if using. Serve with fresh crusty bread.

COOK'S TIP

You can use any small pasta shapes for this soup—try conchigliette or ditalini, or even spaghetti broken up into small pieces. To make a fun soup for children, you could add animal-shaped or alphabet pasta.

VARIATION

Broccoli flowerets can be used to replace the cauliflower flowerets. Substitute 2 tablespoons chopped fresh mixed herbs for the dried mixed herbs.

Cream of Chicken Soup

Serves 4

INGREDIENTS

4 tablespoons unsalted butter
1 large onion, peeled and chopped
10½ ounces cooked chicken,
    shredded finely

2½ cups chicken stock
1 tablespoon chopped fresh tarragon
⅔ cup heavy cream
salt and pepper

fresh tarragon leaves, to garnish
deep fried croûtons, to serve

1 Melt the butter in a large saucepan and fry the onion for 3 minutes.

2 Add the chicken to the saucepan with 1¼ cups of the chicken stock.

3 Bring to a boil and simmer for 20 minutes. Let cool, then process until smooth.

4 Add the remainder of the stock and season with salt and pepper.

5 Add the chopped tarragon, pour the soup into a tureen or individual serving bowls, and add a swirl of cream.

6 Garnish the soup with fresh tarragon and serve with deep-fried croûtons.

VARIATION

To make garlic croûtons, crush 3–4 garlic cloves in a pestle and mortar and add to the oil.

VARIATION

If you can't find fresh tarragon, dried tarragon makes an excellent substitute. Light cream can be used instead of the heavy cream.

Cream of Chicken & Tomato Soup

Serves 2

INGREDIENTS

4 tablespoons sweet butter	2¹/₂ cups chicken stock	²/₃ cup heavy cream
1 large onion, chopped	6 medium tomatoes, finely chopped	salt and pepper
1 pound 2 ounces chicken,	pinch of baking soda	fresh basil leaves, to garnish
shredded very finely	1 tablespoon sugar	croûtons, to serve

1 Melt the butter in a large saucepan and fry the onion and shredded chicken for 5 minutes.

2 Add 1¼ cups of the chicken stock to the pan, together with the chopped tomatoes and baking soda.

3 Bring the soup to a boil and simmer for 20 minutes.

4 Let the soup cool, then process in a food processor.

5 Add the remaining chicken stock, season with salt and pepper, then add the sugar. Pour the soup into a tureen and add a swirl of heavy cream. Serve the soup with croûtons and garnish with fresh basil leaves.

COOK'S TIP

For a healthier version of this soup, use light cream instead of the heavy cream and omit the sugar.

VARIATION

For an Italian-style soup, add 1 tablespoon chopped fresh basil with the stock in step 2. Alternatively, add ¹/₂ teaspoon curry powder or chili powder to make a spicier version of this soup.

Brown Lentil Soup with Pasta

Serves 4

INGREDIENTS

4 slices bacon, cut into small squares	2 celery stalks, chopped	5 cups hot ham or vegetable stock
1 onion, chopped	1/4 cup farfalline or spaghetti broken into small pieces	2 tbsp chopped, fresh mint
2 garlic cloves, crushed	14 1/2 ounce can brown lentils, drained	

1 Place the bacon in a large skillet together with the onions, garlic, and celery. Dry fry for 4–5 minutes, stirring, until the onion is tender and the bacon is just beginning to brown.

2 Add the farfalline or spaghetti pieces to the skillet and cook, stirring, for about 1 minute to coat the pasta in the oil.

3 Add the lentils and the stock and bring to a boil. Reduce the heat and simmer for 12–15 minutes or until the pasta is tender.

4 Remove the skillet from the heat and stir in the chopped fresh mint.

5 Transfer the soup to warm soup bowls and serve immediately.

COOK'S TIP

If you prefer to use dried lentils, add the stock before the pasta and cook for 1–1 1/4 hours, until the lentils are tender. Add the pasta and cook for a further 12–15 minutes.

VARIATION

Any type of pasta can be used in this recipe. Try fusilli, conchiglie, or rigatoni, if you wish.

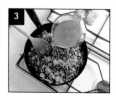

Vegetable Soup with Cannellini Beans

Serves 4

INGREDIENTS

1 small eggplant	3¾ cups hot vegetable or chicken	¼ cup vermicelli
2 large tomatoes	stock	3 tbsp pesto
1 potato, peeled	2 tsp dried basil	freshly grated Parmesan cheese, to
1 carrot, peeled	½ ounce dried porcini mushrooms,	serve (optional)
1 leek	soaked for 10 minutes in	
14½ ounce can cannellini beans	enough warm water to cover	

1 Using a sharp knife, slice the eggplant into rings about ½ inch thick, then cut each ring into 4.

2 Cut the tomatoes and potato into small dice. Cut the carrot into sticks, about 1 inch long and cut the leek into rings.

3 Place the cannellini beans and their liquid in a large saucepan. Add the eggplant, tomatoes, potatoes, carrot, and leek, stirring to mix.

4 Add the stock to the pan and bring to a boil. Reduce the heat and simmer for 15 minutes.

5 Add the basil, dried mushrooms, their soaking liquid, and the vermicelli and simmer for 5 minutes or until all the vegetables are tender.

6 Remove the pan from the heat and stir in the pesto.

7 Ladle into bowls and serve with freshly grated Parmesan cheese, if using.

COOK'S TIP

Porcini mushrooms are grown in southern Italy. When dried and rehydrated they have a very intense flavor, so although they are expensive to buy, only a small amount is required to add flavor to soups or risottos.

Creamy Tomato Soup

Serves 4

INGREDIENTS

3 tbsp butter
1 pound 9 ounces ripe tomatoes,
    preferably plum, roughly
    chopped

3¾ cups hot vegetable stock
⅔ cup milk or light cream
¼ cup ground almonds
1 tsp sugar

2 tbsp shredded basil leaves
salt and pepper

1 Melt the butter in a large saucepan. Add the tomatoes and cook for 5 minutes, until the skins start to wrinkle. Season to taste with salt and pepper.

2 Add the stock to the pan, bring to a boil, cover, and simmer for 10 minutes.

3 Meanwhile, under a preheated broiler, lightly toast the ground almonds until they are golden brown. This will take only 1–2 minutes, so watch them closely.

4 Remove the soup from the heat, place in a food processor, and blend the mixture to form a smooth consistency. Alternatively, mash the soup with a potato masher.

5 Pass the soup through a strainer to remove any tomato skin or seeds.

6 Place the soup in the pan and return to the heat. Stir in the milk or cream, ground almonds, and sugar. Warm the soup through and add the shredded basil just before serving.

7 Transfer the creamy tomato soup to warm soup bowls and serve hot.

VARIATION

Very fine breadcrumbs can be used instead of the ground almonds, if desired. Toast them in the same way as the almonds and add with the milk or cream in step 6.

Tuscan Onion Soup

Serves 4

INGREDIENTS

¹/3 cup diced pancetta
1 tbsp olive oil
4 large white onions, thinly sliced
   in rings

3 garlic cloves, chopped
3³/4 cups hot chicken or ham stock
4 slices ciabatta or other
   Italian bread

3 tbsp butter
2³/4 ounces Swiss or cheddar
   cheese
salt and pepper

1 Dry fry the pancetta in a large saucepan for 3–4 minutes, until it just begins to brown. Remove the pancetta from the saucepan and set aside until required.

2 Add the oil to the pan and sauté the onions and garlic over a high heat for 4 minutes. Reduce the heat, cover, and cook for 15 minutes, until lightly caramelized.

3 Add the stock to the saucepan and bring to a boil. Reduce the heat and simmer, covered, for about 10 minutes.

4 Toast the slices of ciabatta on both sides, under a preheated broiler, for 2–3 minutes, or until golden. Spread the ciabatta with butter and top with the Swiss or cheddar cheese. Cut the bread into bite-size pieces.

5 Add the reserved pancetta to the soup and season to taste with salt and pepper. Pour into 4 soup bowls and top with the toasted bread.

COOK'S TIP

Pancetta is similar to bacon, but it is air- and salt-cured for about 6 months. Pancetta is available from most delicatessens and some large supermarkets. If you cannot obtain pancetta, use unsmoked bacon instead.

Green Soup

Serves 4

1 tbsp olive oil

1 onion, chopped

1 garlic clove, chopped

7 ounces potatoes, peeled and cut into 1-inch cubes

3 cups vegetable or chicken stock

1 small cucumber or ½ large cucumber, cut into chunks

3 ounce bunch watercress

4½ ounces green beans, trimmed and halved lengthwise

salt and pepper

1 Heat the oil in a large pan and sauté the onion and garlic for 3–4 minutes, or until softened. Add the cubed potatoes and cook for a further 2–3 minutes.

2 Stir in the stock, bring to a boil, and simmer for 5 minutes.

3 Add the cucumber to the pan and cook for a further 3 minutes, or until the potatoes are tender. Test by inserting the tip of a knife into the potato cubes—it should pass through easily.

4 Add the watercress and allow to wilt. Then place the soup in a food processor and blend until smooth. Alternatively, before adding the watercress, mash the soup with a potato masher and push through a strainer, then chop the watercress finely and stir into the soup.

5 Bring a small pan of water to a boil and steam the beans for 3–4 minutes, or until tender.

6 Add the beans to the soup, season, and warm through.

VARIATION

Try using 4½ ounces of snow peas instead of the beans, if you prefer.

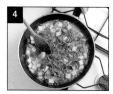

Orange, Thyme, & Pumpkin Soup

Serves 4

INGREDIENTS

2 tbsp olive oil
2 medium onions, chopped
2 cloves garlic, chopped
7 cups diced pumpkin

$6^{1}/_{4}$ cups boiling vegetable or
   chicken stock
finely grated rind and juice of
   1 orange

3 tbsp fresh thyme, stalks removed
$^{2}/_{3}$ cup milk
salt and pepper
crusty bread, to serve

1 Heat the olive oil in a large saucepan. Add the onions to the pan and sauté for 3–4 minutes, or until softened. Add the garlic and pumpkin and cook for a further 2 minutes, stirring well.

2 Add the boiling vegetable or chicken stock, orange rind and juice, and 2 tablespoons of the thyme to the pan. Simmer, covered, for 20 minutes, or until the pumpkin is tender.

3 Place the mixture in a food processor and blend until smooth. Alternatively, mash the mixture with a potato masher until smooth. Season to taste with salt and pepper.

4 Return the soup to the saucepan and add the milk. Reheat the soup for 3–4 minutes, or until it is piping hot, but not boiling. Sprinkle with the remaining fresh thyme just before serving.

5 Divide the soup between 4 warm soup bowls and serve with lots of fresh crusty bread.

COOK'S TIP

Pumpkins are usually large vegetables. To make things a little easier, buy a piece weighing about 2 pounds. Alternatively, make double the quantity and freeze the soup for up to 3 months.

Minestrone

Serves 4

INGREDIENTS

1 tbsp olive oil
²/₃ cup diced pancetta
2 medium onions, chopped
2 cloves garlic, crushed
1 potato, peeled and cut into
　¹/₂-inch cubes
1 carrot, peeled and cut into chunks
1 leek, sliced into rings

¹/₄ green cabbage, shredded
1 celery stalk, chopped
1 pound can chopped tomatoes
7 ounce can small navy beans,
　drained and rinsed
2¹/₂ cups hot ham or chicken stock
　diluted with 2¹/₂ cups
　boiling water

bouquet garni (2 bay leaves, 2
　sprigs rosemary, and 2 sprigs
　thyme, tied together)
salt and pepper
freshly grated Parmesan cheese,
　to serve

1 Heat the oil in a large saucepan. Add the diced pancetta, chopped onions, and garlic, and sauté for about 5 minutes, or until the onions are soft and golden.

2 Add the prepared potato, carrot, leek, cabbage, and celery to the saucepan. Cook for a further 2 minutes, stirring frequently to coat all the vegetables in the oil.

3 Add the tomatoes, small navy beans, hot ham or chicken stock, and bouquet garni to the pan, stirring to mix. Lower the heat and simmer the soup, covered, for 15–20 minutes, or until all the vegetables are just tender.

4 Remove the bouquet garni, season with salt and pepper to taste, and serve with plenty of freshly grated Parmesan.

VARIATION

Any combination of vegetables will work equally well in this soup. For a special minestrone, try adding ¹/₂ cup shredded prosciutto in step 1.

Calabrian Mushroom Soup

Serves 4

INGREDIENTS

2 tbsp olive oil

1 onion, chopped

1 pound mixed mushrooms, such as
    ceps, oyster, and button

1¼ cups milk

3¾ cups hot vegetable stock

8 slices of rustic bread or French
    bread

3 tbsp butter, melted

2 garlic cloves, crushed

¾ cup finely grated Swiss cheese

salt and pepper

1 Heat the oil in a large skillet and sauté the onion for 3–4 minutes, or until soft and golden.

2 Wipe each mushroom with a damp cloth and cut any large mushrooms into smaller, bite-size pieces.

3 Add the mushrooms to the pan, stirring quickly to coat them in the oil.

4 Add the milk to the pan, bring to a boil, cover, lower the heat, and simmer for about 5 minutes.

Gradually stir in the hot vegetable stock.

5 Under a preheated broiler, toast the bread on both sides until golden.

6 Mix together the garlic and butter and spoon generously over the toast.

7 Place the toast in the bottom of a large tureen or divide it between 4 individual serving bowls and pour in the hot soup. Top with the grated Swiss cheese and serve at once.

COOK'S TIP

Mushrooms absorb liquid, which can lessen the flavor and affect cooking properties. Wipe them with a damp cloth rather than rinsing them in water.

VARIATION

Supermarkets stock a wide variety of exotic mushrooms. If you prefer, use a combination of cultivated and exotic mushrooms.

Chicken & Corn Soup

Serves 4

INGREDIENTS

1 pound boned chicken breasts,
cut into strips

5 cups chicken stock

⁵/₈ cup heavy cream

³/₄ cup dried vermicelli

1 tbsp cornstarch

3 tbsp milk

6 ounces corn kernels

salt and pepper

1 Put the chicken, stock, and cream into a large saucepan and slowly bring to a boil. Reduce the heat slightly and simmer for about 20 minutes. Season to taste.

2 Meanwhile, cook the vermicelli in lightly salted boiling water for 10-12 minutes, until just tender. Drain the pasta and keep warm.

3 In a small bowl, mix together the cornstarch and milk to make a smooth paste. Stir the cornstarch paste into the soup until thickened.

4 Add the corn and vermicelli to the saucepan and heat through.

5 Transfer the soup to a warm tureen or individual soup bowls and serve immediately.

COOK'S TIP

If you are short of time, buy ready-cooked chicken, remove any skin, and cut it into slices.

VARIATION

For crab and corn soup, substitute 1 pound cooked crabmeat for the chicken breasts. Flake the crabmeat thoroughly before adding it to the saucepan and reduce the cooking time by 10 minutes. For a Chinese-style soup, substitute egg noodles for the vermicelli and use canned, creamed corn.

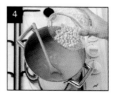

Mussel & Potato Soup

Serves 4

INGREDIENTS

1 pound 10 ounces mussels
2 tbsp olive oil
7 tbsp unsalted butter
2 slices bacon, chopped
1 onion, chopped
2 garlic cloves, crushed
1/2 cup all-purpose flour
1 pound potatoes, thinly sliced

3/4 cup dried conchigliette
1 1/4 cups heavy cream
1 tbsp lemon juice
2 egg yolks
salt and pepper

TO GARNISH:
2 tbsp finely chopped fresh
  parsley
lemon wedges

1 Debeard the mussels and scrub them under cold water for 5 minutes. Discard any mussels that do not close immediately when sharply tapped.

2 Bring a large pan of water to a boil, add the mussels, oil, and a little pepper and cook until the mussels open.

3 Drain the mussels, reserving the cooking liquid. Discard any mussels that are closed. Remove the mussels from their shells.

4 Melt the butter in a large saucepan and cook the bacon, onion, and garlic for 4 minutes. Carefully stir in the flour and then 5 cups of the reserved cooking liquid.

5 Add the potatoes to the pan and simmer for 5 minutes. Add the conchigliette and simmer for a further 10 minutes.

6 Add the cream and lemon juice, season to taste, then add the mussels to the pan.

7 Blend the egg yolks with 1-2 tbsp of the remaining cooking liquid, stir into the pan, and cook for 4 minutes.

8 Ladle the soup into warm soup bowls, garnish with the chopped fresh parsley and lemon wedges, and serve.

Italian Fish Soup

Serves 4

INGREDIENTS

4 tbsp butter	5 cups fish stock (see Cook's Tip)	1 1/4 cups heavy cream
1 pound assorted fish fillets, such as red mullet and snapper	3/4 cup dried pasta shapes, such as ditalini or elbow macaroni	salt and black pepper
1 pound prepared seafood, such as squid and shrimp	1 tbsp anchovy extract	crusty brown bread, to serve
8 ounces fresh crabmeat	grated rind and juice of 1 orange	
1 large onion, sliced	1/4 cup dry sherry	
1/4 cup all-purpose flour		

1 Melt the butter in a large saucepan and cook the fish fillets, seafood, crabmeat, and onion over a low heat for 6 minutes.

2 Stir the flour into the mixture.

3 Gradually stir in the fish stock until the soup comes to a boil. Reduce the heat and simmer for 30 minutes.

4 Add the pasta to the saucepan and cook for a further 10 minutes.

5 Stir in the anchovy extract, orange rind, orange juice, sherry, and heavy cream. Season to taste with salt and pepper.

6 Heat the soup until completely warmed through then transfer to warm soup bowls and serve with crusty brown bread.

COOK'S TIP

The heads, tails, trimmings and bones of most non-oily fish can be used to make fish stock. Simmer 2 pounds fish pieces, including heads, in a large saucepan with 5/8 cup white wine, 1 chopped onion, 1 sliced carrot, 1 sliced celery stalk, 4 black peppercorns, 1 bouquet garni, and 7 1/2 cups water for 30 minutes, then strain.

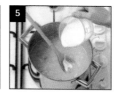

Clear Chicken & Egg Soup

Serves 4

INGREDIENTS

1 tsp salt	4½ ounces broccoli florets	dash of chili sauce
1 tbsp rice wine vinegar	1 cup shredded	chili powder, to garnish
4 eggs	cooked chicken	
3¾ cups chicken stock	2 open-cap mushrooms, sliced	
1 leek, sliced	1 tbsp dry sherry	

1 Bring a large saucepan of water to a boil and add the salt and rice wine vinegar. Reduce the heat so that it is just simmering and carefully break the eggs into the water, one at a time. Poach the eggs for 1 minute. Remove the poached eggs with a slotted spoon and set aside.

2 Bring the chicken stock to a boil in a separate pan and add the leek, broccoli, chicken, mushrooms, and sherry, and season with chili sauce to taste. Cook for 10–15 minutes.

3 Add the poached eggs to the soup and cook for a further 2 minutes. Carefully transfer the soup and poached eggs to 4 individual soup bowls. Dust with a little chili powder to garnish and serve immediately.

VARIATION

You could use 4 dried Chinese mushrooms, rehydrated according to the package instructions, instead of the open-cap mushrooms, if desired.

COOK'S TIP

You could substitute 4½ ounces fresh or canned crab meat or the same quantity of fresh or frozen cooked shrimp for the chicken, if desired.

Curried Chicken & Corn Soup

Serves 4

INGREDIENTS

6 ounce can corn, drained

3³/₄ cups chicken stock

12 ounces cooked, lean chicken, cut
   into strips

16 baby corncobs

1 tsp Chinese curry powder

¹/₂-inch piece fresh ginger
   root, grated

3 tbsp light soy sauce

2 tbsp chopped chives

1 Place the canned corn in a food processor, together with ⅔ cup of the chicken stock and process until the mixture forms a smooth purée.

2 Rub the corn purée through a fine strainer, pressing with the back of a spoon to remove any husks.

3 Pour the remaining chicken stock into a large saucepan and add the strips of cooked chicken. Stir in the corn purée.

4 Add the baby corncobs and bring the soup to a boil. Boil the soup for 10 minutes.

5 Add the curry powder, grated ginger, and soy sauce and cook for a further 10–15 minutes. Stir in the chopped chives.

6 Transfer the soup to warm individual soup bowls and serve immediately.

COOK'S TIP

Prepare the soup up to 24 hours in advance without adding the chicken, cool, cover, and store in the refrigerator. Add the chicken and heat the soup through thoroughly before serving.

Hot & Sour Soup

Serves 4

INGREDIENTS

2 tbsp cornstarch
4 tbsp water
2 tbsp light soy sauce
3 tbsp rice wine vinegar
$^{1}/_{2}$ tsp ground black pepper

1 small fresh red chili,
   finely chopped
1 egg
2 tbsp vegetable oil
1 onion, chopped

$3^{3}/_{4}$ cups chicken or beef
   consommé
1 open-cap mushroom, sliced
$1^{3}/_{4}$ ounces skinless chicken breast,
   cut into very thin strips
1 tsp sesame oil

1 Blend the cornstarch with the water to form a smooth paste. Add the soy sauce, rice wine vinegar, pepper, and chili and mix together well.

2 Break the egg into a separate bowl and beat well.

3 Heat the oil in a preheated wok and stir-fry the onion for 1–2 minutes.

4 Stir in the consommé, mushroom, and chicken and bring to a boil. Cook for about 15 minutes, or until the chicken is tender.

5 Pour the cornstarch mixture into the soup and cook the soup, stirring constantly, until it has thickened.

6 As you are stirring, gradually drizzle the egg into the soup, to create threads of egg.

COOK'S TIP

Make sure that the egg is poured in very slowly and that you stir continuously to create threads of egg and not large pieces.

7 Sprinkle with the sesame oil and serve immediately.

Beef & Vegetable Noodle Soup

Serves 4

INGREDIENTS

8 ounces lean beef	8 ounces egg noodles	4 1/2 ounces broccoli, cut
1 garlic clove, crushed	3 3/4 cups beef stock	into florets
2 scallions, chopped	3 baby corncobs, sliced	pinch of chili powder
3 tbsp soy sauce	1/2 leek, shredded	
1 tsp sesame oil		

1 Using a sharp knife, cut the beef into very thin strips and place them in a shallow glass bowl or dish.

2 Add the garlic, scallions, soy sauce, and sesame oil and mix together well, turning the beef to coat. Cover and marinate in the refrigerator for 30 minutes.

3 Cook the noodles in a saucepan of boiling water for 3–4 minutes. Drain the noodles thoroughly and set aside until they are required.

4 Put the beef stock in a large saucepan and bring to a boil.

5 Add the beef, together with the marinade, the baby corn, leek, and broccoli. Cover and simmer over a low heat for 7–10 minutes, or until the beef and vegetables are tender and cooked through.

6 Stir in the noodles and chili powder and cook for a further 2–3 minutes. Transfer to bowls and serve immediately.

COOK'S TIP

Vary the vegetables used, or use those on hand. If desired, use a few drops of chili sauce instead of chili powder, but remember it is very hot!

Lamb & Rice Soup

Serves 4

INGREDIENTS

5¹/₂ ounces lean lamb
¹/₄ cup rice
3³/₄ cups lamb stock
1 leek, sliced

1 garlic clove, thinly sliced
2 tsp light soy sauce
1 tsp rice wine vinegar

1 medium open-cap mushroom,
  thinly sliced

salt

1 Using a sharp knife, trim any fat from the lamb and cut the meat into thin strips. Set aside until required.

2 Bring a large pan of lightly salted water to a boil and add the rice. Bring back to a boil, stir once, reduce the heat, and cook for 10–15 minutes, until tender. Drain, rinse under cold running water, drain again, and set aside until required.

3 Meanwhile, put the lamb stock in a large saucepan and bring to a boil.

4 Add the lamb strips, leek, garlic, soy sauce, and rice wine vinegar to the stock in the pan. Reduce the heat, cover, and simmer for 10 minutes, or until the lamb is tender and cooked through.

5 Add the mushroom slices and the rice to the pan and cook for a further 2–3 minutes, or until the mushroom is completely cooked through.

6 Ladle the soup into 4 individual warm soup bowls and serve immediately.

COOK'S TIP

Use a few dried Chinese mushrooms, rehydrated according to the package instructions and chopped, as an alternative to the open-cap mushroom. Add the Chinese mushrooms with the lamb in step 4.

Crab & Ginger Soup

Serves 4

INGREDIENTS

1 carrot, peeled and chopped
1 leek, chopped
1 bay leaf
3³/₄ cups fish stock
2 medium-size cooked crabs

1-inch piece fresh ginger root, grated
1 tsp light soy sauce

¹/₂ tsp ground star anise
salt and pepper

1 Put the carrot, leek, bay leaf, and fish stock into a large saucepan and bring to a boil. Reduce the heat, cover, and simmer for about 10 minutes, or until the carrot and leek are nearly tender.

2 Meanwhile, remove all of the meat from the cooked crabs. Break off the claws and legs, break the joints, and remove the meat (you may require a fork for this). Discard the gills, split the bodies open, and scoop out all the meat. Add the crab meat to the saucepan of fish stock.

3 Add the ginger, soy sauce, and star anise to the fish stock and bring to a boil. Simmer for about 10 minutes, or until the vegetables are tender and the crab is heated through. Season to taste with salt and pepper. Ladle the soup into warm individual bowls and serve immediately.

COOK'S TIP

If fresh crab meat is unavailable, use drained canned crab meat or thawed frozen crab meat instead.

COOK'S TIP

To prepare cooked crab, loosen the meat from the shell by banging the back of the underside with a clenched fist. Stand the crab on its edge with the shell toward you. Force the shell from the body with your thumbs. Twist off the legs and claws and remove the meat. Twist off the tail and discard. Remove and discard the gills from each side of the body. Cut the body in half along the center and remove all of the meat. Scoop the brown meat from the shell with a spoon.

Chinese Cabbage Soup

Serves 4

INGREDIENTS

1 pound bok choy	1 tbsp superfine sugar	1 tbsp cornstarch
2¹/₂ cups vegetable stock	1 tbsp dry sherry	2 tbsp water
1 tbsp rice wine vinegar	1 fresh red chili, thinly sliced	
1 tbsp light soy sauce		

1 Using a sharp knife, trim the stems of the bok choy and shred the leaves.

2 Heat the stock in a large saucepan. Add the bok choy and cook for 10–15 minutes.

3 Mix the rice wine vinegar, soy sauce, sugar, and sherry together. Add this mixture to the stock, together with the sliced chili. Bring to a boil, lower the heat, and cook for 2–3 minutes.

4 Blend the cornstarch with the water to form a smooth paste. Gradually stir the cornstarch mixture into the soup. Cook, stirring constantly, until it has thickened. Cook for a further 4–5 minutes. Ladle the soup into individual warm serving bowls and serve immediately.

VARIATION

Boil about 2 tbsp rice in lightly salted water until tender. Drain and spoon into the base of the soup bowls. Ladle the soup over the rice and serve immediately.

COOK'S TIP

Bok choy, also known as pak choi or spoon cabbage, has long, white leaf stalks and fleshy, spoon-shaped, shiny green leaves. There are a number of varieties available, which differ mainly in size rather than flavor.

Coconut & Crab Soup

Serves 4

INGREDIENTS

1 tbsp peanut oil	2¹/₂ cups fish stock	8 ounces fresh or frozen crab claws
2 tbsp Thai red curry paste	2 tbsp fish sauce	2 tbsp chopped fresh cilantro
1 red bell pepper, seeded and sliced	8 ounces canned or fresh white	3 scallions, trimmed and sliced
2¹/₂ cups coconut milk	crab meat	

1 Heat the oil in a large preheated wok.

2 Add the red curry paste and red bell pepper to the wok and stir-fry for 1 minute.

3 Add the coconut milk, fish stock, and fish sauce to the wok and bring to a boil.

4 Add the crab meat (drained if canned), crab claws (thawed if frozen), cilantro, and scallions to the wok. Stir the mixture well and heat thoroughly for 2–3 minutes.

5 Transfer the soup to warm bowls and serve hot.

COOK'S TIP

Coconut milk adds a sweet and creamy flavor to the dish. It is available in powdered form or in cans ready to use.

COOK'S TIP

Clean the wok after each use by washing it with water, using a mild detergent if necessary, and a soft cloth or brush. Do not scrub or use any abrasive cleaner, as this will scratch the surface. Dry thoroughly with paper towels or over a low heat, then wipe the surface all over with a little oil. This forms a sealing layer to protect the surface of the wok from moisture and prevents it rusting.

Chili Fish Soup

Serves 4

INGREDIENTS

1/2 ounce Chinese dried mushrooms	1 1/2 cups bamboo shoots	2 tbsp fresh cilantro
2 tbsp sunflower oil	3 tbsp sweet chili sauce	1 pound cod fillet, skinned and cubed
1 onion, sliced	5 cups fish or vegetable stock	
1 1/2 cups snow peas	3 tbsp light soy sauce	

1 Place the mushrooms in a large bowl. Pour over enough boiling water to cover and let stand for 5 minutes. Drain the mushrooms thoroughly. Using a sharp knife, remove the stalks and roughly chop the caps.

2 Heat the sunflower oil in a preheated wok. Add the onion to the wok and stir-fry for 5 minutes, or until softened.

3 Add the snow peas, bamboo shoots, chili sauce, stock, and soy sauce to the wok and bring to a boil.

4 Add the cilantro and cubed fish to the wok. Lower the heat slightly and simmer for about 5 minutes, or until the fish is cooked through.

5 Transfer the soup to warm bowls, garnish with extra cilantro, if wished, and serve hot.

VARIATION

Cod is used in this recipe, as it is a meaty white fish. For real luxury, use monkfish tail instead.

COOK'S TIP

There are many different varieties of dried mushrooms, but shiitake are best. They are not cheap, but a small quantity will go a long way.

Sweet Potato & Onion Soup

Serves 4

INGREDIENTS

2 tbsp vegetable oil

2 pounds sweet potatoes, diced

1 carrot, diced

2 onions, sliced

2 garlic cloves, crushed

2¹/₂ cups vegetable stock

1¹/₄ cups unsweetened orange juice

1 cup unsweetened yogurt

2 tbsp chopped fresh cilantro

salt and pepper

TO GARNISH:

cilantro sprigs

orange rind

1 Heat the vegetable oil in a large saucepan and add the diced sweet potatoes and carrot, sliced onions, and garlic. Sauté gently for 5 minutes, stirring constantly.

2 Add the vegetable stock and orange juice and bring to a boil.

3 Reduce the heat to a simmer, cover the saucepan, and cook the vegetables for 20 minutes or until the sweet potato and carrot cubes are tender.

4 Transfer the mixture to a food processor or blender in batches and process for 1 minute until puréed. Return the purée to the rinsed-out saucepan.

5 Stir in the unsweetened yogurt and chopped cilantro and season to taste. Serve the soup garnished with cilantro sprigs and orange rind.

COOK'S TIP

This soup can be chilled before serving, if preferred. If chilling it, stir the yogurt into the dish just before serving. Serve in chilled bowls.

Indian Potato & Pea Soup

Serves 4

INGREDIENTS

2 tbsp vegetable oil	1 tsp ground coriander	4 tbsp unsweetened yogurt
8 ounces mealy potatoes, diced	1 tsp ground cumin	salt and pepper
1 large onion, chopped	3³/₄ cups vegetable stock	chopped fresh cilantro, to garnish
2 garlic cloves, crushed	1 red chili, chopped	
1 tsp garam masala	1 cup frozen peas	

1 Heat the vegetable oil in a large saucepan and add the diced potatoes, onion, and garlic. Sauté gently for about 5 minutes, stirring constantly.

2 Add the ground spices and cook for 1 minute, stirring all the time.

3 Stir in the vegetable stock and chopped red chili and bring the mixture to a boil. Reduce the heat, cover the pan, and simmer for 20 minutes, until the potatoes begin to break down.

4 Add the peas and cook for a further 5 minutes. Stir in the yogurt and season to taste.

5 Pour into warm soup bowls, garnish with chopped fresh cilantro, and serve hot with warm bread.

COOK'S TIP

Potatoes blend perfectly with spices, this soup being no exception. For an authentic Indian dish, serve this soup with warm naan bread.

VARIATION

For slightly less heat, seed the chili before adding it to the soup. Always wash your hands after handling chiles as they contain volatile oils that can irritate the skin and make your eyes burn if you touch your face.

Potato, Cabbage, & Chorizo Soup

Serves 4

INGREDIENTS

2 tbsp olive oil	1 garlic clove, crushed	$\frac{1}{2}$ cup sliced chorizo sausage
3 large potatoes, cubed	$4\frac{1}{2}$ cups pork or vegetable stock	salt and pepper
2 red onions, quartered	$1\frac{1}{2}$ cups shredded Savoy cabbage	paprika, to garnish

1 Heat the olive oil in a large saucepan and add the cubed potatoes, quartered red onions, and garlic. Sauté gently for 5 minutes, stirring constantly.

2 Add the pork or vegetable stock and bring to a boil. Reduce the heat and cover the saucepan. Simmer the vegetables for about 20 minutes, until the potatoes are tender.

3 Process the soup in a food processor or blender in 2 batches for 1 minute each. Pour the puréed soup into a clean pan.

4 Add the shredded Savoy cabbage and sliced chorizo sausage to the pan and cook for a further 7 minutes. Season to taste.

5 Ladle the soup into warm soup bowls, garnish with a sprinkling of paprika, and serve.

COOK'S TIP

Chorizo sausage requires no pre-cooking. In this recipe, it is added toward the end of the cooking time so that it does not to overpower the other flavors in the soup.

VARIATION

If chorizo sausage is not available, you could use any other spicy sausage or even salami in its place.

Chinese Potato & Pork Broth

Serves 4

INGREDIENTS

4¹/₂ cups chicken stock	4 tbsp water	3 scallions, sliced thinly
2 large potatoes, diced	1 tbsp light soy sauce	1 red bell pepper, sliced
2 tbsp rice wine vinegar	1 tsp sesame oil	8 ounce can bamboo shoots,
4¹/₂ ounces pork tenderloin, sliced	1 carrot, cut into very thin strips	drained
2 tbsp cornstarch	1 tsp fresh ginger root, chopped	

1 Add the stock, diced potatoes, and 1 tbsp of the rice wine vinegar to a saucepan and bring to a boil. Reduce the heat until the stock is just simmering.

2 In a small bowl, mix the cornstarch with the water. Stir the cornstarch mixture into the hot stock.

3 Bring the stock back to a boil, stirring until thickened, then reduce the heat until it is just simmering again.

4 Place the pork slices in a shallow dish and season with the remaining rice wine vinegar, soy sauce, and sesame oil.

5 Add the pork slices, carrot strips, and chopped ginger to the stock and cook for 10 minutes. Stir in the sliced scallions, red bell pepper, and bamboo shoots. Cook for a further 5 minutes.

6 Pour the soup into warm bowls and serve immediately.

COOK'S TIP

Sesame oil is very strongly flavored and is, therefore, only used in small quantities.

VARIATION

For extra heat, add 1 chopped red chili or 1 tsp chili powder to the soup in step 5.

Celery, Stilton, & Walnut Soup

Serves 4

INGREDIENTS

4 tablespoons butter	2¹⁄₂ cups vegetable stock	2 tablespoons walnut halves,
2 shallots, chopped	1¹⁄₄ cups milk	roughly chopped
3 celery stalks, chopped	1¹⁄₂ cups crumbled blue Stilton	²⁄₃ cup unsweetened yogurt
1 garlic clove, crushed	cheese, plus extra to garnish	salt and pepper
2 tablespoons all-purpose flour		chopped celery leaves, to garnish

1 Melt the butter in a large saucepan and sauté the shallots, celery, and garlic for 2–3 minutes, stirring constantly, until softened.

2 Add the all-purpose flour and cook, stirring constantly, for 30 seconds.

3 Gradually stir in the stock and milk and bring to a boil.

4 Reduce the heat to a gentle simmer and add the crumbled blue Stilton cheese and walnut halves. Cover and simmer for 20 minutes.

5 Stir in the unsweetened yogurt and heat for a further 2 minutes without boiling.

6 Season the soup to taste with salt and pepper, then transfer to a warm soup tureen or individual serving bowls, garnish with chopped celery leaves and extra crumbled blue Stilton cheese, and serve at once.

COOK'S TIP

As well as adding protein, vitamins, and useful fats to the diet, nuts add important flavor and texture to vegetarian meals.

VARIATION

Use an alternative blue cheese, such as Dolcelatte or Gorgonzola, if desired, or a strong vegetarian Cheddar cheese, grated.

Red Bell Pepper & Chili Soup

Serves 4

INGREDIENTS

8 oz red bell peppers,
    seeded and sliced
1 onion, sliced

2 garlic cloves, crushed
1 green chili, chopped
1½ cups sieved tomatoes

2½ cups vegetable stock
2 tablespoons chopped basil
fresh basil sprigs, to garnish

1 Put the bell peppers in a large, heavy-based saucepan, together with the onion, garlic, and chili. Add the sieved tomatoes and vegetable stock and bring to a boil, stirring well.

2 Reduce the heat to a simmer and cook for 20 minutes, or until the bell peppers have softened. Drain, reserving the liquid and vegetables separately.

3 Press the vegetables through a strainer with the back of a wooden spoon. Alternatively, put them in a food processor and process until smooth.

4 Return the vegetable purée to a clean saucepan with the reserved cooking liquid. Add the basil and heat through until hot. Garnish the soup with fresh basil sprigs and serve.

COOK'S TIP

Basil is a useful herb to grow at home. It can be grown easily in a window box.

VARIATION

This soup is also delicious served chilled with ⅔ cup of unsweetened yogurt swirled into it.

Dhal Soup

Serves 4

INGREDIENTS

2 tablespoons butter	1 teaspoon ground cumin	1¼ cups coconut milk
2 garlic cloves, crushed	2¼ pounds canned, chopped	salt and pepper
1 onion, chopped	tomatoes, drained	chopped cilantro and lemon slices,
½ teaspoon turmeric	1 cup red lentils	to garnish
1 teaspoon garam masala	2 teaspoons lemon juice	naan bread, to serve
¼ teaspoon chili powder	2½ cups vegetable stock	

1 Melt the butter in a large saucepan and sauté the garlic and onion for 2–3 minutes, stirring. Add the spices and cook for a further 30 seconds.

2 Stir in the tomatoes, red lentils, lemon juice, vegetable stock, and coconut milk and bring to a boil.

3 Reduce the heat and simmer for 25–30 minutes, until the lentils are tender and cooked.

4 Season to taste and spoon the soup into a warm tureen. Garnish with cilantro and lemon and serve with warm naan bread.

COOK'S TIP

You can buy cans of coconut milk from supermarkets and specialty grocers. Coconut milk is also available in a lighter, reduced-fat version.

COOK'S TIP

Add small quantities of hot water to the pan while the lentils are cooking if they begin to absorb too much of the liquid.

Tuscan Bean & Vegetable Soup

Serves 4

INGREDIENTS

1 medium onion, chopped
1 garlic clove, finely chopped
2 celery stalks, sliced
1 large carrot, diced
14 ounce can chopped
tomatoes

²/₃ cup Italian dry
red wine
5 cups fresh vegetable stock
1 tsp dried oregano
15 ounce can mixed beans
and legumes

2 medium zucchini, diced
1 tbsp tomato paste
salt and pepper

TO SERVE:
low-fat pesto sauce
crusty bread

1 Place the prepared onion, garlic, celery, and carrot in a large saucepan. Stir in the tomatoes, red wine, vegetable stock, and oregano.

2 Bring the vegetable mixture to a boil, cover the pan, and simmer for about 15 minutes. Stir the beans and zucchini into the mixture, and continue to cook, uncovered, for a further 5 minutes.

3 Add the tomato paste and season well with salt and pepper to taste. Then heat through, stirring occasionally, for a further 2–3 minutes, but do not allow the mixture to boil again.

4 Ladle the soup into warm bowls and serve with a spoonful of low-fat pesto on each portion and accompanied with lots of fresh crusty bread.

VARIATION

For a more substantial soup, add 12 ounces diced lean cooked chicken or turkey with the tomato paste in step 3.

Fresh Figs with Prosciutto

Serves 4

INGREDIENTS

1½ ounces arugula	4 tbsp olive oil	1 tbsp clear honey
4 fresh figs	1 tbsp fresh orange juice	1 small red chili
4 slices prosciutto		

1 Tear the arugula into fairly small pieces and arrange on 4 serving plates.

2 Using a sharp knife, cut each of the figs into quarters and place them on top of the arugula leaves.

3 Using a sharp knife, cut the prosciutto into strips and scatter over the arugula and figs.

4 Place the oil, orange juice, and honey in a screw-top jar. Shake the jar vigorously until the mixture emulsifies and forms a thick dressing. Transfer to a serving bowl.

5 Using a sharp knife, dice the chili, remembering not to touch your face before you have washed your hands (see Cook's Tip, right). Add the chopped chili to the dressing and mix well.

6 Drizzle the dressing over the prosciutto, arugula, and figs, tossing to mix well. Serve the salad at once.

COOK'S TIP

Chiles can burn the skin for several hours after chopping, so it is advisable to wear gloves when you are handling the very hot varieties.

COOK'S TIP

Parma, in the Emilia-Romagna region of Italy, is famous for its ham, prosciutto di Parma, *thought to be the best in the world.*

Cured Meats with Olives & Tomatoes

Serves 4

INGREDIENTS

4 plum tomatoes	2 tbsp capers, drained and rinsed	1 tbsp extra-virgin olive oil
1 tbsp balsamic vinegar	1 cup pitted green olives	salt and pepper
6 canned anchovy fillets, drained and rinsed	6 ounces mixed, cured meats, sliced	crusty bread, to serve
	8 fresh basil leaves	

1 Using a sharp knife, cut the tomatoes into evenly sized slices. Sprinkle the tomato slices with the balsamic vinegar and a little salt and pepper to taste and set aside.

2 Chop the anchovy fillets into pieces measuring about the same length as the olives.

3 Push a piece of anchovy and a caper into each olive.

4 Arrange the sliced meat on 4 individual serving plates together with the tomatoes, filled olives, and basil leaves.

5 Lightly drizzle the olive oil over the sliced meat, tomatoes, and olives.

6 Serve the cured meats, olives, and tomatoes with lots of fresh crusty bread.

COOK'S TIP

Fill a screw-top jar with the stuffed olives, cover with olive oil, and use when required—they will keep for one month in the refrigerator.

COOK'S TIP

The cured meats for this recipe are up to your individual taste. They can include a selection of prosciutto, pancetta, bresaola (dried salt beef), and salame di Milano (pork and beef sausage).

Garbanzo Beans with Prosciutto

Serves 4

INGREDIENTS

1 tbsp olive oil	1 small red bell pepper, seeded and	14 ounce can garbanzo beans,
1 medium onion, thinly sliced	cut into thin strips	drained and rinsed
1 garlic clove, chopped	1¼ cups chopped prosciutto	1 tbsp chopped parsley, to garnish
		crusty bread, to serve

1 Heat the oil in a large skillet. Add the sliced onion, chopped garlic, and sliced bell pepper and sauté for 3–4 minutes, or until the vegetables have softened.

2 Add the prosciutto to the skillet and fry with the vegetables for 5 minutes, or until the prosciutto is just beginning to brown.

3 Add the garbanzo beans to the skillet and cook, stirring, for 2–3 minutes, until warmed through.

4 Sprinkle with chopped parsley and transfer to warm serving plates. Serve with lots of fresh crusty bread.

COOK'S TIP

Whenever possible, use fresh herbs when cooking. They are becoming more readily available, especially since the introduction of "growing" herbs, small pots of herbs that you can buy from the supermarket and grow at home. This ensures the herbs are fresh and also provides a continuous supply.

VARIATION

Try adding a small finely diced chili in step 1 for a spicier taste, if desired.

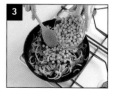

Deep-Fried Seafood

Serves 4

INGREDIENTS

7 ounces prepared squid	1/3 cup all-purpose flour	TO SERVE:
7 ounces raw tiger shrimp, peeled	1 tsp dried basil	garlic mayonnaise (see Cook's Tip)
5 1/2 ounces whitebait	salt and pepper	lemon wedges
oil, for deep-frying		

1 Carefully rinse the squid, shrimp, and whitebait under cold running water, in order to completely removing any dirt or grit.

2 Using a very sharp knife, slice the squid into rings, leaving the tentacles whole.

3 Heat the oil in a large pan until a cube of bread browns in 30 seconds —the oil will then be hot enough for deep-frying.

4 Place the flour in a bowl and season with the salt, pepper, and basil.

5 Roll the squid, shrimp, and whitebait in the seasoned flour until coated all over. Carefully shake off any excess flour.

6 Cook the seafood in the hot oil in batches for 2–3 minutes, or until crispy and golden all over. Remove the seafood with a slotted spoon and drain thoroughly on paper towels. Keep warm while you cook the remaining batches of seafood.

7 Transfer the deep-fried seafood to serving plates and serve with garlic mayonnaise (see Cook's Tip) and lemon wedges.

COOK'S TIP

To make garlic mayonnaise for serving with the deep-fried seafood, crush 2 garlic cloves, stir into 8 tablespoons of mayonnaise, and season with salt and pepper and a little chopped parsley.

Bruschetta with Tomatoes

Serves 4

INGREDIENTS

10^1/$_2$ ounces cherry tomatoes	16 fresh basil leaves, shredded	salt and pepper
4 sun-dried tomatoes	2 garlic cloves, peeled	
4 tbsp extra-virgin olive oil	8 slices ciabatta	

1 Using a sharp knife, cut the cherry tomatoes in half.

2 Using a sharp knife, slice the sun-dried tomatoes into strips.

3 Place the cherry tomatoes and sun-dried tomatoes in a bowl. Add the olive oil and the shredded basil leaves and toss to mix well. Season to taste with a little salt and pepper.

4 Using a sharp knife, cut the garlic cloves in half. Lightly toast the ciabatta bread.

5 Rub the garlic, cut-side down, over both sides of the toasted ciabatta bread.

6 Top the ciabatta bread with the tomato mixture and serve immediately.

COOK'S TIP

Ciabatta is an Italian rustic bread which is slightly holed and quite chewy. It is very good in this recipe as it absorbs the full flavor of the garlic and extra-virgin olive oil.

VARIATION

Plum tomatoes are also good in this recipe. Halve them, then cut them into wedges. Mix them with the sun-dried tomatoes in step 3.

Casserole of Beans in Tomato Sauce

Serves 4

INGREDIENTS

14 ounce can cannellini beans	1 celery stalk	1 pound tomatoes
14 ounce can borlotti beans	2 garlic cloves, chopped	2³/₄ ounces arugula
2 tbsp olive oil	6 ounces baby onions, halved	

1 Drain both cans of beans and reserve 6 tbsp of the liquid.

2 Heat the oil in a large pan. Add the celery, garlic, and onions and sauté for 5 minutes, or until the onions are golden.

3 Cut a cross in the base of each tomato and plunge them into a bowl of boiling water for 30 seconds, until the skins split. Remove them with a slotted spoon and leave until cool enough to handle. Peel off the skin and chop the flesh. Add the tomato flesh and the reserved bean liquid to the pan and cook for 5 minutes.

4 Add the beans to the pan and cook for a further 3–4 minutes, or until the beans are hot.

5 Stir in the arugula and allow to wilt slightly before serving.

VARIATION

For a spicier-tasting dish, add 1–2 teaspoons hot pepper sauce with the beans in step 4.

COOK'S TIP

Another way to peel tomatoes is to cut a cross in the base, then push it onto a fork, and hold it over a flame, turning it slowly so that the skin heats evenly all over. The skin will start to bubble and split, and should then slide off easily.

Tuscan Chicken Livers on Toast

Serves 4

INGREDIENTS

2 tbsp olive oil

1 garlic clove, finely chopped

8 ounces fresh or frozen chicken
   livers, thawed

2 tbsp white wine

2 tbsp lemon juice

4 fresh sage leaves, finely chopped
   or 1 tsp dried, crumbled sage

salt and pepper

4 slices ciabatta or other Italian
   bread

wedges of lemon, to garnish

1 Heat the olive oil in a skillet and sauté the garlic for 1 minute.

2 Rinse and roughly chop the chicken livers, using a sharp knife.

3 Add the chicken livers to the skillet, together with the white wine and lemon juice. Cook for 3–4 minutes, or until the juices from the chicken livers run clear.

4 Stir in the sage and season to taste with salt and pepper.

5 Toast the bread under a preheated broiler for 2 minutes on both sides, or until golden brown.

6 Spoon the hot chicken livers on top of the toasted bread and serve garnished with a wedge of lemon.

COOK'S TIP

Overcooked liver is dry and tasteless. Cook the chopped liver for only 3–4 minutes — it should be soft and tender.

VARIATION

Another way to make crostini is to slice a crusty loaf or a French loaf into small rounds or squares. Heat the olive oil in a skillet and fry the slices of bread until golden brown and crisp on both sides. Remove the crostini from the pan with a slotted spoon and drain thoroughly on paper towels. Top with the chicken livers.

Sesame Shrimp Toasts

Serves 4

INGREDIENTS

8 ounces cooked, peeled shrimp	1 egg white, beaten	4 tbsp sesame seeds
1 scallion		vegetable oil, for deep-frying
¼ tsp salt		
1 tsp light soy sauce	3 thin slices white bread,	
1 tbsp cornstarch	crusts removed	

1 Put the shrimp and scallion in a food processor and process until finely ground. Alternatively, chop them very finely. Transfer to a bowl and stir in the salt, soy sauce, cornstarch, and egg white.

2 Spread the mixture onto one side of each slice of bread. Spread the sesame seeds on top of the mixture, pressing down well.

3 Cut each slice of coated bread into four equal triangles or into strips.

4 Heat the oil for deep-frying in a wok until almost smoking. Carefully place the triangles in the oil, coated side down, and cook for 2–3 minutes, until golden brown. Remove with a slotted spoon and drain on paper towels. Transfer to a serving dish and serve hot.

COOK'S TIP

If desired, you could add ½ tsp very finely chopped fresh ginger root and 1 tsp Chinese rice wine to the shrimp mixture at the end of step 1.

VARIATION

Fry the triangles in two batches, keeping the first batch warm while you cook the second, to prevent them from sticking together and overcooking.

Chinese Omelet

Serves 4

INGREDIENTS

8 eggs	12 jumbo shrimp, peeled and	2 tsp light soy sauce
2 cups cooked chicken, shredded	deveined	dash of chili sauce
	2 tbsp chopped chives	2 tbsp vegetable oil

1 Lightly beat the eggs in a large mixing bowl.

2 Add the shredded chicken and jumbo shrimp to the eggs, mixing well.

3 Stir in the chopped chives, soy sauce, and chili sauce, mixing well.

4 Heat the oil in a large skillet over a medium heat and add the egg mixture, tilting the skillet to coat the base completely. Cook over a medium heat, gently stirring the omelet with a fork occasionally, until the surface is just set and the underside is a golden brown color.

5 When the omelet is set, slide it out of the skillet with a spatula.

6 Cut the omelet into squares or slices to serve.

VARIATION

You could add extra flavor to the omelet by stirring in 3 tablespoons finely chopped fresh cilantro or 1 teaspoon sesame seeds with the chives in step 3.

COOK'S TIP

Add peas or other vegetables to the omelet and serve as a main course for 2 people.

Seven-Spice Eggplants

Serves 4

INGREDIENTS

1 pound eggplants, wiped
1 egg white

7 tbsp cornstarch
1 tsp salt

1 tbsp Thai seven-spice seasoning
oil, for deep-frying

1 Using a sharp knife, slice the eggplants into fairly thin rounds.

2 Place the egg white in a small bowl and beat until light and foamy.

3 Mix together the cornstarch, salt, and seven-spice powder on a large plate.

4 Heat the oil for deep-frying in a large wok.

5 Dip each piece of eggplant into the beaten egg white, then coat in the cornstarch and seven-spice mixture.

6 Deep-fry the coated eggplant slices, in batches, for about 5 minutes, or until pale golden brown and crispy.

7 Transfer the eggplants to absorbent paper towels to drain thoroughly. Transfer the slices to serving plates and serve hot.

COOK'S TIP

The best oil to use for deep-frying is peanut oil which has a high smoke point and mild flavor, so it will neither burn or taint the food. About 2½ cups oil is sufficient.

COOK'S TIP

Thai seven-spice seasoning can be found on the spice shelves of most large supermarkets.

Crispy Seaweed

Serves 4

INGREDIENTS	
2¼ pounds bok choy	1 tsp salt
peanut oil, for deep frying	1 tbsp sugar
(about 3¾ cups)	½ cup toasted pine nuts

1 Rinse the bok choy leaves under cold running water, then pat dry thoroughly with absorbent paper towels.

2 Roll each bok choy leaf up, then slice through thinly so that the leaves are finely shredded.

3 Heat the oil in a large wok. Add the shredded leaves and fry for about 30 seconds, or until they shrivel up and become crispy (you may need to do this in about 4 batches).

4 Remove the crispy seaweed from the wok with a slotted spoon and set aside to drain on absorbent paper towels.

5 Transfer the crispy seaweed to a large bowl and toss with the salt, sugar, and pine nuts. Serve immediately.

VARIATION

Use savoy cabbage instead of the bok choy if it is unavailable, making sure the leaves are well dried before frying.

COOK'S TIP

As a time-saver, you can use a food processor to shred the bok choy finely. Make sure you use only the best leaves; sort through the bok choy and discard any tough, outer leaves, as these will spoil the overall taste and texture of the dish.

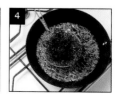

Spicy Chicken Livers with Bok Choy

Serves 4

INGREDIENTS

12 ounces chicken livers	2 cloves garlic, crushed	1 tsp cornstarch
2 tbsp sunflower oil	2 tbsp tomato ketchup	1 pound bok choy
1 red chili, seeded and finely chopped	3 tbsp sherry	egg noodles, to serve
1 tsp fresh grated ginger	3 tbsp soy sauce	

1 Using a sharp knife, trim the fat from the chicken livers and slice them into small pieces.

2 Heat the oil in a large preheated wok. Add the chicken liver pieces and stir-fry over a high heat for 2–3 minutes.

3 Add the chili, ginger, and garlic and stir-fry for about 1 minute.

4 Mix together the tomato ketchup, sherry, soy sauce, and cornstarch in a small bowl and set aside.

5 Add the bok choy to the wok and stir-fry until it just wilts.

6 Add the reserved tomato ketchup mixture to the wok and cook, stirring to mix, until the juices start to bubble.

7 Transfer to serving bowls and serve hot with noodles.

COOK'S TIP

Fresh ginger root will keep for several weeks in a dry, cool place.

COOK'S TIP

Chicken livers are available fresh or frozen from most supermarkets.

Shrimp & Mushroom Omelet

Serves 4

INGREDIENTS

3 tbsp sunflower oil	4 tbsp cornstarch	³/₄ cup bean sprouts
2 leeks, trimmed and sliced	1 tsp salt	6 eggs
12 ounces raw jumbo shrimp	2¹/₃ cups sliced mushrooms	deep-fried leeks, to garnish (optional)

1 Heat the sunflower oil in a large preheated wok. Add the sliced leeks and stir-fry for about 3 minutes.

2 Rinse the shrimp under cold running water, drain, and then pat thoroughly dry with absorbent paper towels.

3 Mix together the cornstarch and salt in a large bowl.

4 Add the jumbo shrimp to the cornstarch and salt mixture and toss well to coat them all over.

5 Add the coated shrimp to the wok and stir-fry for 2 minutes, or until the shrimp are almost cooked through.

6 Add the mushrooms and bean sprouts to the wok and stir-fry for a further 2 minutes.

7 Lightly beat the eggs with 3 tablespoons of cold water. Pour the egg mixture into the wok and cook until the egg has just set, carefully turning the omelet over once. Turn the omelet out onto a clean board, divide it into

COOK'S TIP

If desired, divide the mixture into 4 once the initial cooking has taken place in step 6 and cook 4 individual omelets.

4 portions, and transfer to warm plates. Serve hot, garnished with deep-fried leeks (if using).

Salt & Pepper Shrimp

Serves 4

INGREDIENTS

2 tsp salt	1 pound peeled raw jumbo shrimp	3 cloves garlic, crushed
1 tsp black pepper	2 tbsp peanut oil	scallions, sliced, to garnish
2 tsp Szechwan peppercorns	1 red chili, seeded and finely chopped	shrimp crackers, to serve
1 tsp sugar	1 tsp freshly grated ginger	

1 Finely grind the salt, black pepper and Szechwan peppercorns in a mortar with a pestle. Mix the salt and pepper mixture with the sugar and set aside until required.

2 Rinse the shrimp under cold running water and pat dry with absorbent paper towels.

3 Heat the oil in a preheated wok. Add the shrimp, chili, ginger, and garlic and stir-fry for 4–5 minutes, or until the shrimp are cooked through and have changed color.

4 Add the salt and pepper mixture to the wok and stir-fry for 1 minute.

5 Transfer to warm serving bowls and garnish with sliced scallion. Serve immediately with shrimp crackers.

COOK'S TIP

Szechuan peppercorns are also known as farchiew. *These wild reddish-brown peppercorns from the Szechuan region of China add an aromatic flavor to a dish.*

COOK'S TIP

Jumbo shrimp are widely available and are not only colorful and tasty, but they have a meaty texture, too. If cooked jumbo shrimp are used, add them with the salt and pepper mixture in step 4—if the cooked shrimp are added any earlier they will toughen up and be inedible.

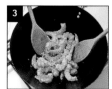

Hummus & Garlic Toasts

Serves 4

INGREDIENTS

HUMMUS:	2 garlic cloves, crushed	TOASTS:
14 oz can garbanzo beans	salt and pepper	1 Italian loaf, sliced
juice of 1 large lemon	chopped fresh cilantro and black	2 garlic cloves, crushed
6 tablespoons sesame seed paste	olives, to garnish	1 tablespoon chopped fresh cilantro
2 tablespoons olive oil		4 tablespoons olive oil

1 To make the hummus, drain the garbanzo beans, reserving a little of the liquid from the can. Put the garbanzo beans and reserved liquid in a food processor and process, gradually adding the lemon juice. Process well after each addition until the mixture is smooth.

2 Stir in the sesame seed paste and all but 1 teaspoon of the olive oil. Add the garlic, season to taste with salt and pepper and process again until smooth.

3 Spoon the hummus into a serving dish. Drizzle the remaining olive oil over the top and garnish with chopped cilantro and olives. Chill in the refrigerator while you are preparing the toasts.

4 Lay the slices of Italian bread on a broiler rack in a single layer.

5 Mix the garlic, cilantro, and olive oil together and drizzle the mixture over the bread slices. Cook under a preheated broiler for 2–3 minutes, until golden brown, turning once. Serve at once with the hummus.

COOK'S TIP

Make the hummus 1 day in advance, and chill, covered, in the refrigerator until required. Garnish and serve.

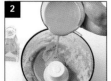

Mixed Bean Pâté

Serves 4

INGREDIENTS

14 oz can mixed beans, drained	juice of 1 lemon	2 scallions, chopped
2 tablespoons olive oil	2 garlic cloves, crushed	salt and pepper
	1 tablespoon chopped fresh cilantro	shredded scallions, to garnish

1 Rinse the beans thoroughly under cold running water and drain well.

2 Transfer the beans to a food processor or blender and process until smooth. Alternatively, place the beans in a bowl and mash with a fork or potato masher.

3 Add the olive oil, lemon juice, crushed garlic, chopped cilantro, and scallions and process or mix thoroughly until fairly smooth. Season with salt and pepper to taste.

4 Transfer the pâté to a serving bowl and chill for at least 30 minutes. Garnish with shredded scallions and serve at once.

COOK'S TIP

Use canned beans which have no salt or sugar added and always rinse thoroughly before use.

COOK'S TIP

Serve the pâté with warm pita bread or toast.

Carrot, Fennel, & Potato Medley

Serves 4

INGREDIENTS

2 tablespoons olive oil

1 potato, cut into thin strips

1 fennel bulb, cut into thin strips

2 carrots, grated

1 red onion, cut into thin strips

chopped chives and fennel fronds, to garnish

DRESSING:

3 tablespoons olive oil

1 tablespoon garlic wine vinegar

1 garlic clove, crushed

1 teaspoon Dijon mustard

2 teaspoons clear honey

salt and pepper

1 Heat the olive oil in a skillet, add the potato and fennel slices, and cook for 2–3 minutes, until beginning to brown. Remove the vegetables from the skillet with a slotted spoon and drain on paper towels.

2 Arrange the carrot, red onion, potato, and fennel in separate piles on a serving platter.

3 Mix the dressing ingredients together and pour over the vegetables. Toss well and sprinkle with chopped chives and fennel fronds. Serve immediately or leave in the refrigerator until required.

COOK'S TIP

Fennel is an aromatic plant that has a delicate, aniseed flavor. It can be eaten raw in salads, or boiled, braised, sautéed, or broiled. For this salad, if fennel is unavailable, substitute 12 ounces sliced leeks.

Paprika Potato Chips

Serves 4

INGREDIENTS

2 large potatoes
3 tbsp olive oil

¹/₂ tsp paprika pepper
salt

1 Using a sharp knife, slice the potatoes very thinly so that they are almost transparent. Drain the potato slices thoroughly and pat dry with paper towels.

2 Heat the oil in a large skillet and add the paprika, stirring constantly, to ensure that the paprika doesn't catch and burn on the bottom of the pan.

3 Add the potato slices to the skillet and cook them in a single layer for about 5 minutes, or until the potato slices just begin to brown and curl slightly at the edges.

4 Remove the potato slices from the pan using a slotted spoon. Transfer them to paper towels and pat dry to drain thoroughly.

5 Thread the potato slices on to several wooden kabob skewers.

6 Sprinkle the potato slices with a little salt and cook over a medium hot barbecue or under a preheated broiler for 10 minutes, turning frequently, until the potato slices begin to crispen. Sprinkle with a little more salt, if desired, and serve.

VARIATION

You could use curry powder or any other spice to flavor the chips instead of the paprika, if desired.

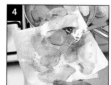

Chicken Pan Bagna

Serves 6

INGREDIENTS

1 long French loaf	³/₄ oz can anchovy fillets	8 large, pitted black olives, chopped
1 garlic clove	12 ounces cold roast chicken	pepper
¹/₂ cup olive oil	2 large tomatoes, sliced	

1 Using a sharp bread knife, cut the French bread in half lengthwise and open out.

2 Cut the garlic clove in half and rub over the bread.

3 Sprinkle the cut surface of the bread with the olive oil.

4 Drain the anchovies and set aside.

5 Thinly slice the chicken and arrange on top of the bread with the sliced tomatoes and drained anchovies.

6 Scatter with the chopped black olives and plenty of black pepper. Sandwich the loaf back together and wrap tightly in foil until required. Cut into slices to serve.

COOK'S TIP

Arrange a few fresh basil leaves in between the tomato slices to add a warm, spicy flavor. Use a good quality olive oil in this recipe for extra flavor.

VARIATION

Instead of putting sliced tomatoes in the sandwich you could rub half a tomato over the cut surface of the bread, squeezing out all the pulp and discarding the skin. Then sprinkle with the olive oil.

Salads & Snacks

As a side dish or a light meal, salads are a healthy and delicious choice. They provide a variety of nutritional benefits while being quick and easy to prepare. There are many ingredients that you can combine to create a colorful and flavorsome dish. If you are looking to create an Italian taste, Tuscan Bean Salad with Tuna is an excellent choice; alternatively, the taste of the Orient can be found in Indonesian Potato and Chicken Salad. If you require a vegetarian selection, there are many recipes to choose from, including Beetroot and Orange Rice Salad, Coconut Couscous Salad, and the simple, but delicious, Mushroom Salad.

For an alternative flavor and texture, other quick and tasty snacks have been added for when you want to rustle something different up. All will satisfy your hunger as well as your taste-buds. The rich variety of easy-to-make dishes includes Mexican-Style Pizzas, Tagliarini with Gorgonzola, and Rosy Melon and Strawberries—something to cater for every craving and taste.

Tuscan Bean Salad with Tuna

Serves 4

INGREDIENTS

1 small white onion or 2 scallions,
   finely chopped
2 x 14 ounce cans dried lima beans,
   drained

2 medium tomatoes
6½ ounce can tuna, drained
2 tbsp flat leaf parsley, chopped
2 tbsp olive oil

1 tbsp lemon juice
2 tsp clear honey
1 garlic clove, crushed

1 Place the chopped onion or scallions and lima beans in a bowl and mix well to combine.

2 Using a sharp knife, cut the tomatoes into wedges. Add the tomatoes to the onion and bean mixture.

3 Flake the tuna with a fork and add it to the onion and bean mixture, together with the parsley.

4 In a screw-top jar, mix together the olive oil, lemon juice, honey, and garlic. Shake the jar vigorously until the dressing emulsifies and thickens.

5 Pour the dressing over the bean salad. Toss the ingredients together using 2 spoons and serve.

COOK'S TIP

This salad will keep for several days in a covered container in the refrigerator. Make up the dressing just before serving and toss the ingredients together to mix well.

VARIATION

Substitute fresh salmon for the tuna if you wish to create a luxurious version of this recipe for a special occasion.

Italian Potato Salad

Serves 4

INGREDIENTS

1 pound baby potatoes, unpeeled,
or larger potatoes, halved
4 tbsp unsweetened yogurt

4 tbsp mayonnaise
8 sun-dried tomatoes

2 tbsp flat leaf parsley, chopped
salt and pepper

1 Rinse and clean the potatoes and place them in a large pan of water. Bring to a boil and cook for 8–12 minutes, or until just tender. (The cooking time will vary according to the size of your potatoes.)

2 Using a sharp knife, cut the sun-dried tomatoes into thin slices.

3 To make the dressing, mix together the yogurt and mayonnaise in a bowl and season to taste with a little salt and pepper. Stir in the sun-dried tomato slices and the chopped flat leaf parsley.

4 Remove the potatoes with a slotted spoon, drain them thoroughly, and then set them aside to cool. If you are using larger potatoes, cut them into 2-inch chunks.

5 Pour the dressing over the potatoes and toss to mix.

6 Chill the potato salad in the refrigerator for about 20 minutes, then serve as a starter or as an accompaniment.

COOK'S TIP

It is easier to cut the larger potatoes once they are cooked. Although smaller pieces of potato will cook more quickly, they tend to disintegrate and become mushy.

Minted Fennel Salad

Serves 4

INGREDIENTS

1 bulb fennel	1 small or ½ a large cucumber	1 tbsp virgin olive oil
2 small oranges	1 tbsp chopped mint	2 eggs, hard-boiled

1 Using a sharp knife, trim the outer leaves from the fennel bulb. Slice the fennel bulb thinly into a bowl of water and sprinkle with lemon juice (see Cook's Tip).

2 Grate the rind of the oranges over a bowl. Using a sharp knife, pare away the orange pith, then segment the oranges by carefully slicing between each line of pith. Do this over the bowl in order to retain the juice.

3 Using a sharp knife, cut the cucumber into ½-inch slices and then cut each slice into quarters. Add the cucumber to the fennel and orange mixture together with the mint.

4 Pour the olive oil over the fennel and cucumber salad and toss well.

5 Peel and quarter the eggs and use them to decorate the top of the salad. Serve at once.

COOK'S TIP

Virgin olive oil, which has a fine aroma and flavor, is made by the cold pressing of olives. However, it may have a slightly higher acidity level than extra-virgin oil.

COOK'S TIP

Fennel will discolor if it is left for any length of time without a dressing. To prevent any discoloration, place it in a bowl of water and sprinkle with lemon juice.

Mushroom Salad

Serves 4

INGREDIENTS

5½ ounces firm white mushrooms
4 tbsp virgin olive oil

1 tbsp lemon juice
5 anchovy fillets, drained and
chopped

1 tbsp fresh marjoram
salt and pepper

1 Gently wipe each mushroom with a damp cloth to remove any excess dirt. Slice the mushrooms thinly, using a sharp knife.

2 Mix together the olive oil and lemon juice and pour the mixture over the mushrooms. Toss together so that the mushrooms are completely coated with the lemon juice and oil.

3 Stir the chopped anchovy fillets into the mushrooms. Season the mushroom mixture with black pepper and garnish with the fresh marjoram.

4 Let the mushroom salad stand for 5 minutes before serving in order for all the flavors to be absorbed. Season with a little salt (see Cook's Tip, below) and then serve.

COOK'S TIP

Do not season the mushroom salad with salt until the very last minute as it will cause the mushrooms to blacken and the juices to leak. The result will not be as tasty as it should be as the full flavors will not be absorbed and it will look very unattractive.

COOK'S TIP

If you use dried herbs rather than fresh, remember that you need only about one-third of dried to fresh.

Yellow Bell Pepper Salad

Serves 4

INGREDIENTS

4 slices bacon, chopped	1 celery stalk, finely chopped	1 tbsp fresh thyme
2 yellow bell peppers	3 plum tomatoes, cut into wedges	
8 radishes, washed and trimmed	3 tbsp olive oil	

1 Dry fry the chopped bacon in a skillet for 4–5 minutes, or until crispy. Remove the bacon from the skillet, set aside, and cool until required.

2 Using a sharp knife, halve and seed the bell peppers. Slice the bell peppers into long strips.

3 Using a sharp knife, halve the radishes and cut them into wedges.

4 Mix together the bell peppers, radishes, celery, and tomatoes, and toss the mixture in the olive oil and fresh thyme. Season to taste with a little salt and pepper.

5 Transfer the salad to serving plates and garnish with the reserved crispy bacon.

COOK'S TIP

Tomatoes are actually berries and are related to potatoes. There are many different shapes and sizes of this versatile fruit. The one most used in Italian cooking is the plum tomato, which is very flavorsome.

COOK'S TIP

Pre-packaged diced bacon can be purchased from most supermarkets, which helps to save on preparation time.

Lentil & Tuna Salad

Serves 4

INGREDIENTS

3 tbsp virgin olive oil
1 tbsp lemon juice
1 tsp wholegrain mustard
1 garlic clove, crushed

$^1/_2$ tsp ground cumin
$^1/_2$ tsp ground coriander
1 small red onion
2 ripe tomatoes
14 ounce can lentils, drained

$6^1/_2$ can tuna, drained
2 tbsp fresh cilantro, chopped
pepper

1 Using a sharp knife, seed and dice the tomatoes into pieces.

2 Using a very sharp knife, finely chop the red onion.

3 To make the dressing, beat together the virgin olive oil, lemon juice, mustard, garlic, ground cumin, and ground coriander in a small bowl. Set aside until required.

4 Carefully mix together the chopped onion, diced tomatoes, and drained lentils in a large bowl.

5 Flake the tuna and stir it into the onion, tomato, and lentil mixture.

6 Stir in the chopped fresh cilantro.

7 Pour the dressing over the lentil and tuna salad and season with freshly ground black pepper. Serve at once.

COOK'S TIP

Lentils are a good source of protein and contain important vitamins and minerals. Buy them dried for soaking and cooking yourself, or buy canned varieties for speed and convenience.

VARIATION

Nuts would add extra flavor and texture to this salad.

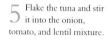

Chinese Shrimp Salad

Serves 4

INGREDIENTS

9 ounces fine egg noodles	3/4 cup bean sprouts	12 ounces peeled cooked shrimp
3 tbsp sunflower oil	1 ripe mango, sliced	2 tbsp light soy sauce
1 tbsp sesame oil	6 scallions, sliced	1 tbsp sherry
1 tbsp sesame seeds	2 3/4 ounces radishes, sliced	

1 Place the egg noodles in a large bowl and pour over enough boiling water to cover. Let stand for 10 minutes.

2 Drain the noodles thoroughly and pat away any moisture with absorbent paper towels.

3 Heat the sunflower oil in a large preheated wok. Add the noodles and stir-fry for 5 minutes, tossing frequently.

4 Remove the wok from the heat and add the sesame oil, sesame seeds, and bean sprouts, tossing to mix well.

5 In a separate bowl, mix together the sliced mango, scallions, radishes, shrimp, light soy sauce, and sherry.

6 Toss the shrimp mixture with the noodles or alternatively, arrange the noodles around the edge of a serving plate and pile the shrimp mixture into the center. Serve immediately.

VARIATION

If fresh mango is unavailable, use canned mango slices, rinsed and drained, instead.

Old English Spicy Chicken Salad

Serves 4

INGREDIENTS

9 ounces young spinach leaves

3 stalks celery, thinly sliced

1/2 cucumber

2 scallions

3 tablespoons chopped fresh parsley

12 ounces boneless, roast chicken,
    thinly sliced

DRESSING:

1-inch piece fresh ginger
    root, finely grated

3 tablespoons olive oil

1 tablespoon white wine vinegar

1 tablespoon honey

1/2 teaspoon ground cinnamon

salt and pepper

smoked almonds,
    to garnish (optional)

1 Thoroughly wash the spinach leaves, then pat dry with paper towels.

2 Using a sharp knife, thinly slice the celery, cucumber, and scallions. Toss in a large bowl, together with the spinach leaves and parsley.

3 Transfer to serving plates and arrange the chicken over the salad.

4 Combine all the dressing ingredients and shake well to mix.

5 Season to taste, then pour onto the salad. Sprinkle with a few smoked almonds, if using.

VARIATION

*Substitute corn
salad for the spinach,
if desired.*

VARIATION

*Fresh young spinach
leaves go particularly
well with fruit–try
adding a few fresh
raspberries or nectarine
slices to make an even
more refreshing salad.*

Potato, Mixed Bean, & Apple Salad

Serves 4

INGREDIENTS

8 ounces new potatoes, scrubbed
and quartered
1²/₃ cups mixed canned beans, such
as red kidney beans, flageolet,
and borlotti beans, drained and
rinsed

1 red eating apple, diced and tossed
in 1 tbsp lemon juice
1 small yellow bell pepper, diced
1 shallot, sliced
¹/₂ bulb fennel, sliced
oak leaf lettuce leaves

DRESSING:
1 tbsp red wine vinegar
2 tbsp olive oil
¹/₂ tbsp American mustard
1 garlic clove, crushed
2 tsp chopped fresh thyme

1 Cook the quartered potatoes in a saucepan of boiling water for 15 minutes, until tender. Drain and transfer to a mixing bowl.

2 Add the mixed beans to the potatoes with the diced apple and yellow bell pepper, and the sliced shallots and fennel. Mix well, taking care not to break up the cooked potatoes.

3 In a bowl, beat all the dressing ingredients together, then pour it on the potato salad.

4 Line a plate or salad bowl with the oak leaf lettuce leaves and spoon the potato mixture into the center. Serve immediately.

COOK'S TIP

Canned beans are used here for convenience, but dried beans may be used instead. Soak for 8 hours or overnight, drain, and place in a saucepan. Cover with water, bring to a boil, and boil for 10 minutes, then simmer until tender.

VARIATION

Use Dijon or wholegrain mustard in place of American mustard for a different flavor.

Potato, Radish, & Cucumber Salad

Serves 4

INGREDIENTS

1 pound new potatoes, scrubbed and halved	1 bunch radishes, sliced thinly	2 tbsp olive oil
½ cucumber, sliced thinly	DRESSING:	1 tbsp white wine vinegar
2 tsp salt	1 tbsp Dijon mustard	2 tbsp mixed chopped herbs

1 Cook the potatoes in a saucepan of boiling water for 10–15 minutes, or until tender. Drain and let cool.

2 Meanwhile spread out the cucumber slices on a plate and sprinkle with the salt. Let stand for 30 minutes, then rinse under cold running water, and pat dry with paper towels.

3 Arrange the cucumber and radish slices on a serving plate in a decorative pattern and pile the cooked potatoes in the center of the slices.

4 In a small bowl, mix the dressing ingredients together. Pour the dressing on the salad, tossing well to coat all the salad ingredients. Chill in the refrigerator before serving.

VARIATION

Dijon mustard has a mild clean taste, which is perfect for this salad as it does not overpower the other flavors. If unavailable, use another mild mustard — English mustard is too strong for this salad.

COOK'S TIP

The cucumber adds not only color, but a real freshness to the salad. It is salted and let stand to remove the excess water which would make the salad soggy. Wash the cucumber well to remove all the salt, before adding to the salad.

Sweet Potato & Nut Salad

Serves 4

INGREDIENTS

1 pound sweet potatoes, diced	1/2 cup chopped pecans	DRESSING:
2 celery stalks, sliced	2 heads endive, separated	4 tbsp vegetable oil
1 cup grated celery root	1 tsp lemon juice	1 tbsp garlic wine vinegar
2 scallions, sliced	thyme sprigs, to garnish	1 tsp light brown sugar
		2 tsp chopped fresh thyme

1 Cook the sweet potatoes in a saucepan of boiling water for 5 minutes, until tender. Drain thoroughly and let cool.

2 When cooled, stir in the celery, celery root, scallions and pecans.

3 Line a salad plate with the endive leaves and sprinkle them with lemon juice.

4 Spoon the potato mixture into the center of the leaves.

5 In a small bowl, beat the dressing ingredients together.

6 Pour the dressing over the salad and serve at once, garnished with thyme sprigs.

VARIATION

For variety, replace the garlic wine vinegar in the dressing with a different flavored vinegar, such as chili or herb.

COOK'S TIP

Sweet potatoes do not store as well as ordinary potatoes. It is best to store them in a cool, dark place (not the refrigerator) and use within 1 week of purchase.

Potato, Arugula, & Apple Salad

Serves 4

INGREDIENTS

2 large potatoes, unpeeled and
  sliced
2 green eating apples, diced
1 tsp lemon juice
$1/4$ cup walnut pieces
$1/2$ cup cubed goat cheese

$5^{1}/2$ ounces arugula leaves
salt and pepper

DRESSING:
2 tbsp olive oil
1 tbsp red wine vinegar

1 tsp clear honey
1 tsp fennel seeds

1 Cook the potatoes in a pan of boiling water for 15 minutes, until tender. Drain and let cool. Transfer the cooled potatoes to a serving bowl.

2 Toss the diced apples in the lemon juice, drain, and stir into the cold potatoes.

3 Add the walnut pieces, cheese cubes, and arugula leaves, then toss the salad to mix.

4 In a small bowl, beat the dressing ingredients together and pour the dressing on the salad. Serve immediately.

VARIATION

Use smoked or blue cheese instead of goat cheese, if you prefer. In addition, if arugula is unavailable use baby spinach instead.

COOK'S TIP

Serve this salad immediately to prevent the apple from discoloring. Alternatively, prepare all the other ingredients in advance and add the apple at the last minute.

Potato & Mixed Vegetable Salad with Lemon Mayonnaise

Serves 4

INGREDIENTS

1 pound waxy new potatoes, scrubbed
1 carrot, cut into matchsticks
8 ounces cauliflower flowerets
8 ounces baby corn cobs, halved lengthwise
6 ounces green beans

1 cup diced ham,
2/3 cup sliced mushrooms
salt and pepper

DRESSING:
2 tbsp chopped fresh parsley
2/3 cup mayonnaise

2/3 cup unsweetened yogurt
4 tsp lemon juice
rind of 1 lemon
2 tsp fennel seeds

1 Cook the potatoes in a pan of boiling water for 15 minutes, or until tender. Drain and let cool. When the potatoes are cold, slice them thinly.

2 Meanwhile, cook the carrot matchsticks, cauliflower flowerets, baby corn cobs, and green beans in a pan of boiling water for 5 minutes. Drain well and let cool.

3 Reserve 1 tsp of the chopped parsley for the garnish. In a bowl, mix the remaining dressing ingredients together.

4 Arrange the vegetables on a salad platter and top with the ham strips and sliced mushrooms.

5 Spoon the dressing over the the salad and garnish with the reserved parsley. Serve at once.

COOK'S TIP

For a really quick salad, use a frozen packet of mixed vegetables, thawed, instead of fresh vegetables.

Indonesian Potato & Chicken Salad

Serves 4

INGREDIENTS

4 large waxy potatoes, diced

10$^1/_2$ ounces fresh pineapple, diced

2 carrots, grated

6 ounces bean sprouts

1 bunch scallions, sliced

1 large zucchini, cut into
   matchsticks

3 celery stalks, cut into matchsticks

1 cup unsalted peanuts

2 cooked chicken breast fillets,
   about 4$^1/_2$ ounces each, sliced

DRESSING:

6 tbsp crunchy peanut butter

6 tbsp olive oil

2 tbsp light soy sauce

1 red chili, chopped

2 tsp sesame oil

4 tsp lime juice

1 Cook the diced potatoes in a saucepan of boiling water for 10 minutes, or until tender. Drain and let cool.

2 Transfer the cooled potatoes to a salad bowl.

3 Add the pineapple, carrots, bean sprouts, scallions, zucchini, celery, peanuts, and sliced chicken to the potatoes. Toss well to mix all the salad ingredients together.

4 To make the dressing, put the peanut butter in a small bowl and gradually beat in the olive oil and light soy sauce.

5 Stir in the chopped red chili, sesame oil, and lime juice. Mix until well combined.

6 Pour the spicy dressing on the salad and toss lightly to coat all the ingredients. Serve the salad immediately, garnished with the lime wedges.

COOK'S TIP

Unsweetened canned pineapple may be used in place of the fresh pineapple for convenience. If only sweetened canned pineapple is available, drain it and rinse under cold running water before using.

Broiled New Potato Salad

Serves 4

INGREDIENTS

1¹/₂ pounds new potatoes, scrubbed	salt and pepper	DRESSING:
3 tbsp olive oil	parsley sprig, to garnish	4 tbsp mayonnaise
2 tbsp chopped fresh thyme		1 tbsp garlic wine vinegar
1 tsp paprika		2 garlic cloves, crushed
4 slices smoked bacon		1 tbsp chopped fresh parsley

1 Cook the new potatoes in a saucepan of boiling water for 10 minutes. Drain thoroughly.

2 Mix the olive oil, chopped thyme, and paprika together and pour the mixture over the warm potatoes.

3 Place the bacon under a preheated broiler and cook for 5 minutes, turning once, until crisp. When thoroughly cooked, roughly chop the bacon and keep warm.

4 Transfer the potatoes to the broiler pan and cook for 10 minutes, turning once.

5 Mix the dressing ingredients in a small serving bowl. Transfer the potatoes and bacon to a large serving bowl. Season with salt and pepper and mix together.

6 Spoon over the dressing, garnish with a parsley sprig, and serve immediately for a warm salad. Alternatively, let cool and serve chilled.

VARIATION

Add spicy sausage to the salad in place of bacon – you do not need to cook it under the broiler before adding to the salad.

Potato & Italian Sausage Salad

Serves 4

INGREDIENTS

1 pound waxy potatoes	1 red onion, halved and sliced	DRESSING:
1 radicchio or lollo rosso lettuce	4 1/2 cups sun-dried tomatoes, sliced	1 tbsp balsamic vinegar
1 green bell pepper, sliced	2 tbsp shredded fresh basil	1 tsp tomato paste
6 ounces Italian sausage, sliced		2 tbsp olive oil
		salt and pepper

1 Cook the potatoes in a saucepan of boiling water for 20 minutes, or until cooked through. Drain and let cool.

2 Line a large serving platter with the radicchio or lollo rosso lettuce leaves.

3 Slice the cooled potatoes and arrange them in layers on the lettuce-lined serving platter, together with the sliced green bell pepper, sliced Italian sausage, red onion, sun-dried tomatoes, and shredded fresh basil.

4 In a small bowl, beat the balsamic vinegar, tomato paste, and olive oil together and season to taste with salt and pepper. Pour the dressing on the potato salad and serve immediately.

COOK'S TIP

You can use either packets of sun-dried tomatoes or jars of sun-dried tomatoes in oil. If using tomatoes packed in oil, simply rinse the oil from the tomatoes and pat them dry on paper towels before using.

VARIATION

Any sliced Italian sausage or salami can be used in this salad. Italy is the home of the salami and there are numerous varieties to choose from—those from the south tend to be more highly spiced than those from the north of the country.

Root Vegetable Salad

Serves 4

INGREDIENTS

12 ounces carrots
8 ounces daikon (white radish)
4 ounces radishes
12 ounces celery root
1 tbsp orange juice
2 celery stalks with leaves,
 washed and trimmed

3¹/₂ ounces assorted salad
 greens
1 ounce chopped walnuts

DRESSING:
1 tbsp walnut oil
1 tbsp white wine vinegar

1 tsp wholegrain mustard
¹/₂ tsp finely grated orange
 rind
1 tsp celery seeds
salt and pepper

1 Peel and coarsely grate or very finely shred the carrots, daikon (white radish), and radishes. Set these vegetables aside in separate bowls until required.

2 Peel and coarsely grate or finely shred the celery root and mix with the orange juice.

3 Remove the celery leaves and reserve for garnishing. Finely chop the celery stalks.

4 Divide the salad greens among 4 serving plates and arrange the carrots, daikon (white radish), and radishes in small piles on top. Set aside while you make the dressing.

5 Mix all of the dressing ingredients together and season with salt and pepper to taste. Drizzle a little of the dressing over each salad. Shred the reserved celery leaves and sprinkle over the salad with the chopped walnuts.

COOK'S TIP

Also known as Chinese white radish and mooli, daikon resembles a large white parsnip. It has crisp, slightly pungent flesh, which can be eaten raw or cooked. It is a useful ingredient in stir-fries. Fresh daikon tend to have a stronger flavor than store-bought ones.

Beet & Orange Rice Salad

Serves 4

INGREDIENTS

1 1/3 cups long-grain and wild
   rices (see Cook's Tip)
4 large oranges
1 pound cooked beet, peeled
2 heads of chicory
salt and pepper

fresh snipped chives, to
   garnish

DRESSING:
4 tbsp low-fat unsweetened
   yogurt
1 garlic clove, crushed

1 tbsp wholegrain mustard
1/2 tsp finely grated orange
   rind
2 tsp clear honey

1 Cook the rices according to the instructions on the packet. Drain and set aside to cool.

2 Slice the top and bottom off each orange and remove the skin and pith. Holding the orange over a bowl to catch the juice, carefully slice between each segment. Place the segments in a separate bowl. Cover the juice and chill in the refrigerator until required.

3 Drain the beet if necessary and dice into cubes. Mix with the orange segments, cover, and chill.

4 When the rice has cooled, mix in the reserved orange juice and season with salt and pepper to taste.

5 Line 4 serving bowls or plates with the chicory leaves. Spoon the rice over the leaves and top with the beet and oranges.

6 Mix all the dressing ingredients together and spoon over the salad, or serve separately in a bowl, if preferred. Garnish with fresh snipped chives.

COOK'S TIP

Look for boxes of ready-mixed long-grain and wild rices. Alternatively, you can cook 1 cup white rice and 1/4 cup wild rice separately.

Red Hot Slaw

Serves 4

INGREDIENTS

½ small red cabbage
1 large carrot
2 red-skinned apples
1 tbsp lemon juice
1 medium red onion
3½ ounces reduced-fat
    Cheddar cheese, grated

TO GARNISH:
red chili strips
carrot strips

DRESSING:
3 tbsp reduced-calorie
    mayonnaise

3 tbsp low-fat unsweetened
    yogurt
1 garlic clove, crushed
1 tsp paprika
1–2 tsp chili powder
pinch cayenne pepper
    (optional)
salt and pepper

1 Cut the red cabbage in half and remove the central core. Finely shred the leaves and place in a large bowl. Peel and coarsely grate or finely shred the carrot and mix into the cabbage.

2 Core the apples and finely dice, leaving on the skins. Place in another bowl and toss in the lemon juice to prevent the apple browning. Mix the apple into the cabbage and carrot.

3 Peel and finely shred or grate the onion. Stir into the other vegetables, along with the cheese, and mix together.

4 To make the dressing, mix together the mayonnaise, yogurt, garlic, and paprika in a small bowl. Add chili powder according to taste, and the cayenne pepper, if using— this will add more spice to the dressing. Season well.

5 Toss the dressing into the vegetables and mix well. Cover and chill in the refrigerator for 1 hour to allow the flavors to develop. Serve garnished with strips of red chili and carrot.

Pasta Niçoise Salad

Serves 4

INGREDIENTS

8 ounces farfalle (pasta bows)
6 ounces green beans, topped and tailed
12 ounces fresh tuna steaks
4 ounces baby plum tomatoes, halved
8 anchovy fillets, drained on absorbent paper towels

2 tbsp capers in water, drained
1 ounce pitted black olives in water, drained
fresh basil leaves, to garnish
salt and pepper

DRESSING:
1 tbsp olive oil
1 garlic clove, crushed
1 tbsp lemon juice
1/2 tsp finely grated lemon rind
1 tbsp shredded fresh basil leaves

1 Cook the pasta in a pan of lightly salted boiling water according to the instructions on the packet until just cooked. Drain well, set aside, and keep warm.

2 Bring a small saucepan of lightly salted water to a boil and cook the green beans for 5–6 minutes, until just tender. Drain well and toss into the pasta. Set aside and keep warm.

3 Preheat the broiler. Rinse and pat the tuna steaks dry on absorbent paper towels. Season on both sides with black pepper. Place the tuna steaks on the broiler rack and cook for 4–5 minutes on each side, until cooked through.

4 Drain the tuna on absorbent paper towels and flake into bite-size pieces. Toss the tuna into the pasta, along with the tomatoes, anchovies, capers, and olives. Set aside and keep warm.

5 Meanwhile, prepare the dressing. Mix all the ingredients together and season well. Pour the dressing over the pasta mixture and mix carefully. Transfer to a warmed serving bowl and serve sprinkled with fresh basil leaves.

Coconut Couscous Salad

Serves 4

INGREDIENTS

12 ounces couscous
6 ounces dried apricots
1 small bunch fresh chives
2 tbsp unsweetened
    shredded coconut
1 tsp ground cinnamon
salt and pepper

shredded mint leaves, to
garnish

DRESSING:
1 tbsp olive oil
2 tbsp unsweetened orange
juice

$^1/_2$ tsp finely grated orange
    rind
1 tsp wholegrain mustard
1 tsp clear honey
2 tbsp chopped fresh mint
    leaves

1 Soak the couscous according to the instructions on the packet.

2 Bring a large pan of water to a boil. Transfer the couscous to a steamer or large strainer lined with cheesecloth and place over the water. Cover and steam as directed. Remove from the heat, place in heatproof bowl, and set aside to cool.

3 Meanwhile, slice the apricots into thin strips

and place in a small bowl. Using kitchen scissors, snip the chives over the apricots.

4 When the couscous is cool, mix in the apricots, chives, coconut, and cinnamon. Season well.

5 To make the dressing, mix all the ingredients together and season. Pour over the couscous and mix until well combined. Cover and leave to chill for 1 hour to allow the flavors to

develop. Serve the salad garnished with shredded mint leaves.

COOK'S TIP

To serve this salad hot, when the couscous has been steamed, mix in the apricots, chives, coconut, cinnamon, and seasoning, along with 1 tbsp olive oil. Transfer to a warmed serving bowl and serve.

Rosy Melon & Strawberries

Serves 4

INGREDIENTS

1/4 honeydew melon
1/2 Charentais or Cantaloupe
melon

2/3 cup rosé wine
2-3 tsp rosewater

6 ounces small strawberries,
washed and hulled
rose petals, to garnish

1 Scoop out the seeds from both melons with a spoon. Then carefully remove the skin, taking care not to remove too much flesh.

2 Cut the melon flesh into thin strips and place in a bowl. Pour in the wine and sufficient rosewater to taste. Mix together gently, cover, and chill in the refrigerator for at least 2 hours.

3 Halve the strawberries and carefully mix into the melon. Allow the melon and strawberries to stand at room temperature for about 15 minutes for the flavors to develop fully.

4 Arrange the melon and strawberries on individual serving plates and serve sprinkled with a few rose petals.

COOK'S TIP

Rosewater is a distillation of rose petals. It is generally available from large pharmacies and leading supermarkets, as well as from more specialty food suppliers.

VARIATION

It does not matter whether the rosé wine is sweet or dry—although sweet wine contains more calories. Experiment with different types of melon. Varieties such as "Sweet Dream" have whitish-green flesh, while Charentais melons, which have orange flesh, are fragrant and go better with a dry wine. If you wish, soak the strawberries in the wine with the melon, but always allow the fruit to return to room temperature before serving.

Spaghetti with Anchovy & Pesto Sauce

Serves 4

INGREDIENTS

3/8 cup olive oil

2 garlic cloves, crushed

2 ounce can anchovy fillets, drained

1 pound dried spaghetti

2 ounces pesto sauce

2 tbsp finely chopped fresh oregano

1 cup grated Parmesan cheese, plus extra for serving (optional)

salt and pepper

2 fresh oregano sprigs, to garnish

1 Reserve 1 tbsp of the oil and heat the remainder in a small saucepan. Add the garlic and fry for 3 minutes.

2 Lower the heat, stir in the anchovies, and cook, stirring occasionally, until the anchovies have disintegrated.

3 Bring a large saucepan of lightly salted water to a boil. Add the spaghetti and the remaining olive oil and cook until just tender.

4 Add the pesto sauce and chopped fresh oregano to the anchovy mixture and then season with black pepper to taste.

5 Drain the spaghetti and transfer to a warm serving dish. Pour over the pesto sauce and then sprinkle over the grated Parmesan cheese, if using.

6 Garnish with oregano sprigs and serve with extra cheese, if using.

VARIATION

For a vegetarian version of this recipe, simply substitute drained sun-dried tomatoes for the anchovy fillets.

COOK'S TIP

If you find canned anchovies much too salty, soak them in a saucer of milk for 5 minutes, drain, and pat dry with paper towels before using them.

Char-Broiled Mediterranean Vegetable Kabobs

Makes 8

INGREDIENTS

1 large red bell pepper
1 large green bell pepper
1 large orange bell pepper
1 large zucchini
4 baby eggplants
2 medium red onions

2 tbsp lemon juice
1 tbsp olive oil
1 garlic clove, crushed
1 tbsp chopped, fresh
    rosemary or 1 tsp dried
salt and pepper

TO SERVE:
cracked wheat, cooked
tomato and olive relish

1 Halve and seed the bell peppers and cut into even sized pieces, about 1 inch wide. Trim the zucchini, cut in half lengthwise, and slice into 1-inch pieces. Place the bell peppers and zucchini into a large bowl and set aside.

2 Using a sharp knife, trim the eggplants and quarter them lengthwise. Peel the onions, then cut each one into 8 even-sized wedges. Add the eggplant and onion pieces to the bowl containing the bell peppers and zucchini.

3 In a small bowl, mix together the lemon juice, olive oil, garlic, rosemary, and salt and pepper to taste. Pour the mixture over the vegetables and stir well to coat.

4 Preheat the broiler. Thread the vegetables onto 8 skewers. Arrange the kabobs on the rack and cook for 10–12 minutes, turning frequently, until the vegetables are lightly charred and just softened.

5 Drain the vegetable kabobs and serve on a bed of cracked wheat accompanied with a tomato and olive relish, if desired.

Mexican-Style Pizzas

Serves 4

INGREDIENTS

4 ready-made individual
    pizza bases
1 tbsp olive oil
7 ounce can chopped
    tomatoes with garlic and
    herbs
2 tbsp tomato paste

7 ounce can kidney beans,
    drained and rinsed
4 ounces corn kernels, thawed
    if frozen
1–2 tsp chili sauce
1 large red onion, shredded

3½ ounces reduced-fat
    cheddar cheese, grated
1 large green chili, sliced into
    rings
salt and pepper

1 Preheat the oven to 425°F. Arrange the pizza bases on a cookie sheet and brush them lightly with the oil.

2 In a bowl, mix together the chopped tomatoes, tomato paste, kidney beans, and corn, and add chili sauce to taste. Season with salt and pepper to taste.

3 Spread the tomato and kidney bean mixture evenly over each pizza base to cover. Top each pizza with shredded onion and sprinkle with some grated cheese and a few slices of green chili according to taste. Bake in the oven for about 20 minutes until the vegetables are tender, the cheese has melted, and the base is crisp and golden.

4 Remove the pizzas from the cookie sheet and transfer to serving plates. Serve immediately.

COOK'S TIP

For a low-fat Mexican-style salad to serve with this pizza, arrange sliced tomatoes, fresh cilantro leaves, and a few slices of a small, ripe avocado. Sprinkle with fresh lime juice and coarse sea salt. Avocados have quite a high oil content, so eat in moderation.

Tagliarini with Gorgonzola

Serves 4

INGREDIENTS

2 tbsp butter
8 ounces Gorgonzola cheese,
    roughly crumbled
$5/8$ cup heavy cream

2 tbsp dry white wine
1 tsp cornstarch
4 fresh sage sprigs, finely
    chopped
14 ounces dried tagliarini

2 tbsp olive oil
salt and white pepper

1 Melt the butter in a saucepan, stir in 6 ounces of the Gorgonzola cheese and melt, over a low heat, for about 2 minutes.

2 Add the cream, wine, and cornstarch to the pan and beat with a whisk until fully incorporated.

3 Stir in the sage and season to taste with salt and white pepper. Bring to a boil over a low heat, whisking constantly, until the sauce thickens. Remove from the heat and set aside.

4 Bring a large pan of lightly salted water to a boil. Add the tagliarini and 1 tbsp of the olive oil. Cook the pasta for 12–14 minutes, or until just tender, drain and toss in the remaining oil. Transfer the pasta to a serving dish and keep warm.

5 Reheat the sauce over a low heat, whisking constantly. Spoon the Gorgonzola sauce over the tagliarini, generously sprinkle with the remaining crumbled cheese, and serve immediately.

COOK'S TIP

Gorgonzola is one of the world's oldest veined cheeses and, arguably, its finest. Always check that it is creamy yellow with delicate green veining. Avoid hard or discolored cheese. It should have a rich, piquant aroma, not a bitter smell. If you find Gorgonzola too strong or rich, substitute a milder blue cheese.

Spaghetti with Ricotta Cheese

Serves 4

INGREDIENTS

12 ounces dried spaghetti	pinch of grated nutmeg	salt and pepper
3 tbsp olive oil	pinch of ground cinnamon	fresh parsley sprigs, to garnish
3 tbsp butter	$5/8$ cup unsweetened yogurt	
2 tbsp chopped fresh parsley	$1/2$ cup hot chicken stock	
1 cup freshly ground almonds	1 tbsp pine nuts	
$1/2$ cup ricotta cheese		

1 Bring a large pan of lightly salted water to a boil. Add the spaghetti and 1 tbsp of the oil and cook until tender, but still firm to the bite.

2 Drain the pasta, return to the pan, and toss with the butter and chopped parsley. Set aside and keep warm.

3 To make the sauce, mix together the ground almonds, ricotta cheese, nutmeg, cinnamon, and unsweetened yogurt over a low heat to form a thick paste. Stir in the remaining oil, then gradually stir in the hot chicken stock, until smooth. Season the sauce with black pepper to taste.

4 Transfer the spaghetti to a warm serving dish, pour the sauce on top, and toss together well (see Cook's Tip). Sprinkle with the pine nuts, garnish with the fresh parsley, and serve the spaghetti warm.

COOK'S TIP

Use two large forks to toss spaghetti or other long pasta, so that it is thoroughly coated with the sauce. Special spaghetti forks are available from some cookware departments and kitchen stores. Holding one fork in each hand, gently ease the prongs under the pasta on each side and lift them toward the center. Continue until the pasta is completely coated.

Vegetable Spaghetti with Lemon Dressing

Serves 4

INGREDIENTS

8 ounces celery root	1 tbsp lemon juice	1 tbsp lemon juice
2 medium carrots	10$\frac{1}{2}$ ounces spaghetti	4 tbsp low-fat unsweetened
2 medium leeks	celery leaves, chopped, to	yogurt
1 small red bell pepper	garnish	2 tbsp snipped fresh chives
1 small yellow bell pepper		salt and pepper
2 garlic cloves	LEMON DRESSING:	
1 tsp celery seeds	1 tsp finely grated lemon rind	

1 Peel the celery root and carrots and cut them into thin matchsticks, using a sharp knife. Place the celery root and carrots in a bowl. Trim and slice the leeks, rinse to flush out any trapped dirt, then shred finely. Halve, seed, and slice the bell peppers. Peel and thinly slice the garlic. Add all of the vegetables to the bowl containing the celery root and the carrots.

2 Toss the vegetables with the celery seeds and lemon juice.

3 Bring a large saucepan of water to a boil and cook the spaghetti according to the instructions on the packet. Drain and keep warm.

4 Meanwhile, bring another large saucepan of water to a boil, put vegetables in a steamer or strainer and place over the boiling water. Cover and steam for 6–7 minutes or until tender.

5 When the spaghetti and vegetables are cooked, mix the ingredients for the lemon dressing together.

6 Transfer the spaghetti and vegetables to a warm serving bowl and mix with the dressing. Garnish with celery leaves and serve.

Stir-Fried Bean Curd with Peanut & Chili Sauce

Serves 4

INGREDIENTS

1 pound bean curd, cubed
oil, for frying

SAUCE:
6 tbsp crunchy peanut butter
1 tbsp sweet chili sauce

²/₃ cup coconut milk
1 tbsp tomato paste
¹/₄ cup chopped salted peanuts

1 Pat away any moisture from the bean curd, using absorbent paper towels.

2 Heat the oil in a large wok until very hot. Cook the bean curd, in batches, for about 5 minutes, or until golden and crispy. Remove the bean curd with a slotted spoon, transfer to absorbent paper towels and set aside to drain.

3 To make the sauce, mix together the crunchy peanut butter, sweet chili sauce, coconut milk, tomato paste, and chopped peanuts in a bowl. Add a little boiling water if necessary to achieve a smooth consistency.

4 Transfer the crispy fried bean curd to serving plates and serve with the peanut and chili sauce.

COOK'S TIP

Cook the peanut and chili sauce in a saucepan over a gentle heat before serving, if desired.

COOK'S TIP

Make sure that all of the moisture has been absorbed from the bean curd before frying, otherwise it will not turn crisp.

Pasta Provençale

Serves 4

INGREDIENTS

8 ounces penne (pasta quills)
1 tbsp olive oil
1 ounce pitted black olives,
   drained and chopped
1 ounce dry-pack sun-dried
   tomatoes, soaked, drained,
   and chopped
14 ounce can artichoke hearts,
   drained and halved

4 ounces baby zucchini,
   trimmed and sliced
4 ounces baby plum
   tomatoes, halved
3 1/2 ounces assorted baby
   salad greens
salt and pepper
shredded basil leaves, to
   garnish

DRESSING:
4 tbsp sieved tomatoes
2 tbsp low-fat unsweetened
   yogurt
1 tbsp unsweetened orange
   juice
1 small bunch fresh basil,
   shredded

1 Cook the penne (pasta quills) according to the instructions on the packet. Do not overcook the pasta—it should still have bite. Drain well and return to the pan. Stir in the olive oil, salt and pepper, olives, and sun-dried tomatoes. Let cool.

2 Gently mix the artichokes, zucchini, and plum tomatoes into the cooked pasta. Arrange the salad greens in a large serving bowl.

3 To make the dressing, mix all the ingredients together until well combined and toss into the vegetables and pasta.

4 Spoon the mixture on top of the salad greens and garnish with shredded basil leaves.

VARIATION

For a nonvegetarian version, stir 8 ounces canned tuna in brine, drained and flaked, into the pasta together with the vegetables. Other pasta shapes can be included—try farfalle (bows) and rotelle (spoked wheels).

Garlic Mushrooms on Toast

Serves 4

INGREDIENTS

6 tablespoons vegetarian margarine	4 cups sliced mixed mushrooms,	8 slices French bread
2 garlic cloves, crushed	such as open-cap, button,	1 tablespoon chopped parsley
	oyster, and shiitake	salt and pepper

1 Melt the margarine in a skillet over medium heat. Add the crushed garlic and cook for 30 seconds, stirring.

2 Add the mushrooms and cook for 5 minutes, turning occasionally.

3 Toast the slices of French bread under a preheated broiler for about 2–3 minutes, turning once.

4 Transfer the toasts to a serving plate.

5 Toss the parsley into the mushrooms, mixing well, and season well with salt and pepper to taste.

6 Spoon the mushroom mixture over the bread and serve at once.

COOK'S TIP

Store mushrooms for 24–36 hours in the refrigerator, in paper bags, as they sweat in plastic. Wild mushrooms should be washed but other varieties can simply be wiped with paper towels.

COOK'S TIP

Add seasonings, such as curry powder or chili powder, to the mushrooms for extra flavor, if desired.

Potato, Bell Pepper, & Mushroom Hash

Serves 4

INGREDIENTS

1½ pounds potatoes, cubed

1 tablespoon olive oil

2 garlic cloves, crushed

1 green bell pepper, cubed

1 yellow bell pepper, cubed

3 tomatoes, diced

1 cup halved button mushrooms

1 tablespoon vegetarian
  Worcestershire sauce

2 tablespoons chopped basil

salt and pepper

fresh basil sprigs, to garnish

warm, crusty bread, to serve

1 Cook the potatoes in a saucepan of boiling, salted water for 7–8 minutes. Drain well and reserve.

2 Heat the olive oil in a large, heavy-based skillet and cook the potatoes for 8–10 minutes, stirring constantly, until they are golden brown.

3 Add the garlic and bell peppers and cook for 2–3 minutes.

4 Stir in the tomatoes and mushrooms and cook, stirring, for 5–6 minutes.

5 Stir in the vegetarian Worcestershire sauce and basil and season well. Garnish and serve with crusty bread.

VARIATION

This dish can also be eaten cold as a salad.

COOK'S TIP

Most brands of Worcestershire sauce contain anchovies, so make sure you choose a vegetarian variety.

Scrambled Bean Curd on Toasted Rolls

Serves 4

INGREDIENTS

6 tablespoons vegetarian margarine
1 pound marinated,
   firm bean curd

1 red onion, chopped
1 red bell pepper, chopped
4 rolls

2 tablespoons chopped mixed herbs
salt and pepper
fresh herbs, to garnish

1 Melt the margarine in a heavy-based skillet over medium heat and crumble the bean curd into the pan.

2 Add the onion and bell pepper and cook for 3–4 minutes, stirring occasionally.

3 Meanwhile, slice the rolls in half and toast under a preheated broiler for about 2–3 minutes, turning once. Remove the toasts and transfer to a serving plate.

4 Add the herbs to the bean curd mixture, combine, and season to taste.

5 Spoon the bean curd mixture onto the toast and garnish with fresh herbs. Serve at once.

COOK'S TIP

Marinated bean curd adds extra flavor to this dish. Smoked bean curd could be used in its place.

COOK'S TIP

Rub the cut surface of a garlic clove over the toasted rolls for extra flavor.

Mixed Bean Pan-Fry

Serves 4

INGREDIENTS

4 cups mixed fresh beans, such as
    green and fava beans
2 tablespoons vegetable oil
2 garlic cloves, crushed

1 red onion, halved
    and sliced
8 ounces firm marinated
    bean curd, diced
1 tablespoon lemon juice

$^1/_2$ teaspoon turmeric
1 teaspoon pumpkin pie spice
$^2/_3$ cup vegetable stock
2 teaspoons sesame seeds

1 Trim and chop the green beans and set aside until they are required.

2 Heat the oil in a skillet over medium heat and sauté the garlic and onion for 2 minutes, stirring well.

3 Add the bean curd and cook for 2–3 minutes, until it is just beginning to brown.

4 Add the green beans and fava beans.
Stir in the lemon juice, turmeric, pumpkin pie spice, and vegetable stock and bring to a boil.

5 Reduce the heat and simmer for 5–7 minutes, or until the beans are tender. Sprinkle with sesame seeds and serve at once.

VARIATION

Add lime juice instead of lemon, for an alternative citrus flavor.

VARIATION

Use smoked bean curd instead of marinated bean curd for an alternative flavor.

Vegetable Pasta Nests

Serves 4

INGREDIENTS

6 ounces spaghetti
1 eggplant, halved and sliced
1 zucchini, diced
1 red bell pepper, seeded and
    sliced diagonally

6 tablespoons olive oil
2 garlic cloves, crushed
4 tablespoons butter or
    vegetarian margarine, melted

1 tablespoon dry white bread
    crumbs
salt and pepper
fresh parsley sprigs, to garnish

1 Bring a large saucepan of water to a boil and cook the spaghetti until "al dente," or according to the instructions on the packet. Drain well and set aside until required.

2 Place the eggplant, zucchini, and bell pepper in a single layer on a cookie sheet.

3 Mix the oil and garlic together and pour the mixture over the vegetables, tossing to coat.

4 Cook under a preheated broiler for about 10 minutes, turning frequently, until tender and lightly charred. Set aside and keep warm.

5 Divide the spaghetti among 4 lightly greased muffin pans. Using a fork, curl the spaghetti to form nests.

6 Brush the pasta nests with melted butter or margarine and sprinkle with the bread crumbs. Bake in a preheated oven, at 400°F for 15 minutes, or until lightly

golden. Remove the pasta nests from the pans and transfer to serving plates. Divide the broiled vegetables among the pasta nests, season, and garnish.

COOK'S TIP

"Al dente" means "to the bite" and describes cooked pasta that is not too soft, but still has a bite to it.

Refried Beans with Tortillas

Serves 4

<hr>

INGREDIENTS

BEANS:

2 tablespoons olive oil

1 onion, finely chopped

3 garlic cloves, crushed

1 green chili, chopped

14 ounce can red kidney
    beans, drained

14 ounce can pinto beans, drained

2 tablespoons chopped cilantro

$^{2}/_{3}$ cup vegetable stock

8 wheat tortillas

$^{1}/_{4}$ cup grated vegetarian
    cheddar cheese

salt and pepper

RELISH:

4 scallions, chopped

1 red onion, chopped

1 green chili, chopped

1 tablespoon garlic wine vinegar

1 teaspoon sugar

1 tomato, chopped

<hr>

1 Heat the oil for the beans in a large skillet. Add the onion and sauté for 3–5 minutes. Add the garlic and chili and cook for 1 minute.

2 Mash the beans with a potato masher and stir into the pan with the cilantro.

3 Stir in the stock and cook the beans, stirring, for 5 minutes, until soft and pulpy.

4 Place the tortillas on a cookie sheet and heat through in a warm oven for about 1–2 minutes.

5 Mix the relish ingredients together.

6 Spoon the beans into a serving dish and top with the cheese. Season well with salt and pepper. Roll the tortillas and serve with the relish and beans.

COOK'S TIP

Add a little more liquid to the beans when they are cooking if they begin to stick to the bottom of the skillet.

Cabbage & Walnut Stir-Fry

Serves 4

INGREDIENTS

12 ounces white cabbage	2 garlic cloves, crushed	1 cup walnut halves
12 ounces red cabbage	8 scallions, trimmed	2 teaspoons Dijon mustard
4 tablespoons peanut oil	8 ounces firm bean curd, cubed	2 teaspoons poppy seeds
1 tablespoon walnut oil	2 tablespoons lemon juice	salt and pepper

1 Using a sharp knife, shred the white and red cabbages thinly and set aside until required.

2 Heat together the peanut oil and walnut oil in a preheated wok. Add the garlic, cabbage, scallions, and bean curd and cook for 5 minutes, stirring.

3 Add the lemon juice, walnuts, and mustard, season with salt and pepper, and cook for a further 5 minutes, or until the cabbage is tender.

4 Transfer the stir-fry to a warm serving bowl, sprinkle with poppy seeds, and serve.

COOK'S TIP

As well as adding protein, vitamins, and useful fats to the diet, nuts and seeds add flavor and texture to vegetarian meals. Keep a good supply of them in your cupboard, as they can be used in a great variety of dishes—salads, bakes, stir-fries, to name but a few.

VARIATION

Sesame seeds could be used instead of the poppy seeds and drizzle 1 teaspoon of sesame oil over the dish just before serving, if desired.

Marinated Broiled Fennel

Serves 4

INGREDIENTS

2 fennel bulbs
1 red bell pepper, cut into large
    cubes
1 lime, cut into eight wedges

MARINADE:
2 tablespoons lime juice
4 tablespoons olive oil
2 garlic cloves, crushed

1 teaspoon whole-grain mustard
1 tablespoon chopped thyme
fennel fronds, to garnish
crisp salad, to serve

1 Cut each of the fennel bulbs into eight pieces and place in a shallow dish. Mix in the bell peppers.

2 To make the marinade, combine the lime juice, oil, garlic, mustard, and thyme. Pour the marinade over the fennel and bell peppers and set aside to marinate for 1 hour.

3 Thread the fennel and bell peppers onto wooden skewers with the lime wedges. Preheat a broiler to medium and broil the kebabs for 10 minutes, turning and basting frequently with the marinade.

4 Transfer to serving plates, garnish with fennel fronds and serve with a crisp salad.

VARIATION

Substitute 2 tablespoons orange juice for the lime juice and add 1 tablespoon honey, if desired.

COOK'S TIP

Soak the skewers in water for 20 minutes before using to prevent them from burning during cooking.

Ciabatta Rolls

Serves 4

INGREDIENTS

4 ciabatta rolls	FILLING:	1 yellow bell pepper
2 tablespoons olive oil	1 red bell pepper	4 radishes, sliced
1 garlic clove crushed	1 green bell pepper	1 bunch watercress
		8 tablespoons cream cheese

1 Slice the ciabatta rolls in half. Heat the olive oil and crushed garlic in a saucepan. Pour the oil mixture over the cut surfaces of the rolls and let stand while you prepare the filling.

2 Halve the bell peppers and place, skin side uppermost, on a broiler rack. Cook under a preheated broiler for about 8–10 minutes, until just beginning to char. Remove the bell peppers from the broiler, peel and thinly slice the flesh.

3 Arrange the radish slices on one half of each roll with a few watercress leaves. Spoon the cream cheese on top. Pile the bell peppers on top of the cream cheese and top with the other half of the roll. Serve.

COOK'S TIP

To peel bell peppers, wrap them in foil after broiling. This traps the steam, loosening the skins, and making them easier to peel.

COOK'S TIP

Allow the bell peppers to cool slightly before filling the rolls, otherwise the cheese will melt.

Tagliatelle with Zucchini Sauce

Serves 4

INGREDIENTS

1 pound 7 ounces zucchini

6 tablespoons olive oil

3 garlic cloves, crushed

3 tablespoons chopped basil

2 red chilies, sliced

juice of 1 large lemon

5 tablespoons light cream

4 tablespoons freshly grated
Parmesan cheese

8 ounces tagliatelle

salt and pepper

salad greens and grated Parmesan
cheese, to serve (optional)

1 Using a vegetable peeler, slice the zucchini into very thin ribbons.

2 Heat the oil in a skillet and sauté the garlic for about 30 seconds.

3 Add the zucchini and cook over gentle heat, stirring, for 5–7 minutes.

4 Stir in the basil, chilies, lemon juice, light cream, and grated Parmesan cheese and season with salt and pepper to taste.

5 Meanwhile, cook the tagliatelle in a large pan of lightly salted boiling water for 10 minutes, until "al dente." Drain the pasta thoroughly and transfer to a warm serving bowl.

6 Pile the zucchini mixture on top of the pasta. Serve at once with salad greens and extra Parmesan, if desired.

VARIATION

Lime juice and zest could be used instead of the lemon as an alternative.

Olive, Bell Pepper, & Cherry Tomato Pasta

Serves 4

INGREDIENTS

2 cups penne

2 tablespoons olive oil

2 tablespoons butter

2 garlic cloves, crushed

1 green bell pepper, thinly sliced

1 yellow bell pepper, thinly sliced

16 cherry tomatoes, halved

1 tablespoon chopped oregano

1/2 cup dry white wine

2 tablespoons quartered, pitted
   black olives

2³/₄ ounces arugula

salt and pepper

fresh oregano sprigs, to garnish

1 Cook the pasta in a saucepan of boiling salted water for 8–10 minutes, or until "al dente." Drain thoroughly.

2 Heat the oil and butter in a pan until the butter melts. Sauté the garlic for 30 seconds. Add the bell peppers and cook for 3–4 minutes, stirring.

3 Stir in the cherry tomatoes, oregano, wine, and olives and cook

for 3–4 minutes. Season well with salt and pepper and stir in the arugula until just wilted.

4 Transfer the pasta to a serving dish, spoon over the sauce, and mix well. Garnish and serve.

COOK'S TIP

Ensure that the saucepan is large enough to prevent the pasta from sticking together during cooking.

194

Spinach & Pine Nut Pasta

Serves 4

8 ounces pasta shapes or spaghetti

1/2 cup olive oil

2 garlic cloves, crushed

1 onion, quartered and sliced

3 large flat mushrooms, sliced

8 ounces spinach

2 tablespoons pine nuts

6 tablespoons dry white wine

salt and pepper

Parmesan shavings, to garnish

1 Cook the pasta in a saucepan of boiling salted water for 8–10 minutes, or until "al dente." Drain well.

2 Meanwhile, heat the oil in a large saucepan and sauté the garlic and onion for 1 minute.

3 Add the sliced mushrooms and cook for 2 minutes, stirring occasionally.

4 Add the spinach and cook for 4–5 minutes, or until the spinach has wilted.

5 Stir in the pine nuts and wine, season well with salt and pepper, and cook for 1 minute.

6 Transfer the pasta to a warm serving bowl and toss the sauce into it, mixing well. Garnish with shavings of Parmesan cheese and serve at once.

COOK'S TIP

Freshly grate a little nutmeg over the dish for extra flavor, as it is particularly good with spinach.

Bean Curd & Vegetable Stir-Fry

Serves 4

| INGREDIENTS |

1¼ cups diced potatoes
1 tablespoon olive oil
1 red onion, sliced
8 ounces firm bean curd, diced

2 zucchini, diced
8 canned artichoke hearts, halved
²/₃ cup sieved tomatoes

1 teaspoon sugar
2 tablespoons chopped basil
salt and pepper

1 Cook the potatoes in a saucepan of boiling water for 10 minutes. Drain thoroughly and set aside until required.

2 Heat the oil in a large skillet and sauté the red onion for 2 minutes, until the onion has softened, stirring.

3 Stir in the bean curd and zucchini and cook for 3–4 minutes, until they begin to brown slightly. Add the potatoes, stirring to mix.

4 Stir in the artichoke hearts, sieved tomatoes, sugar, and basil, season with salt and pepper, and cook for a further 5 minutes, stirring well. Transfer the stir-fry to serving dishes and serve.

COOK'S TIP

Canned artichoke hearts should be drained thoroughly and rinsed before use because they often have salt added.

VARIATION

Eggplants could be used instead of the zucchini, if desired.

Meat & Poultry

The variety of ways in which meat and poultry can be cooked are included to create a sumptuous selection of dishes. Barbeques, stir-fries, roasts, and casseroles are combined to offer a wealth of textures and flavors. Classic and traditional recipes feature alongside more exotic dishes taken from all around the world, incorporating exciting new ingredients alongside family favorites.

For the poultry-lover there are pasta dishes, risottos, and bakes, incorporating a variety of healthy and colorful ingredients. For those who enjoy Asian cuisine, choose from Chili Chicken, Honey-Glazed Duck, Pork Fry with Vegetables, and Lamb with Mushroom Sauce. All of these recipes are mouth-watering, as well as quick and easy to prepare.

The dishes in this chapter range from easy, economic mid-week suppers to sophisticated and elegant main courses for special occasions. All of the recipes are extremely wholesome, offering a comprehensive range of tastes. Those on a low-fat diet should choose lean cuts of meat and look for low-fat ground beef to enjoy the dishes featured here.

Chicken & Spinach Salad

Serves 4

INGREDIENTS

4 boneless, skinless chicken
  breasts, 5^1/$_2$ ounces each
2 cups fresh chicken stock
1 bay leaf
8 ounces fresh young
  spinach leaves
1 small red onion, shredded

4 ounces fresh raspberries
salt and freshly ground
  pink peppercorns
fresh toasted croûtons, to
  garnish

DRESSING:
4 tbsp low-fat unsweetened
  yogurt
1 tbsp raspberry vinegar
2 tsp clear honey

1 Place the chicken breasts in a skillet. Add the chicken stock and the bay leaf. Bring to a boil, cover, and simmer for 15–20 minutes, turning halfway through, until the chicken is completely cooked through. Allow to cool in the liquid.

2 Arrange the spinach leaves on 4 serving plates and top with the shredded red onion. Cover and leave to chill in the refrigerator.

3 Drain the cooked chicken and pat dry on absorbent paper towels. Slice the chicken breasts thinly and arrange, fanned out, over the spinach and onion. Sprinkle with the raspberries.

4 To make the dressing, mix all the ingredients together in a small bowl.

5 Drizzle a spoonful of dressing over each chicken breast and season with salt and ground pink

peppercorns to taste. Serve the salad with freshly toasted croûtons.

VARIATION

This recipe is delicious with smoked chicken, but it will be more expensive and richer, so use slightly less. It would make an impressive starter for a dinner party.

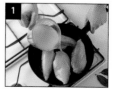

Harlequin Chicken

Serves 4

INGREDIENTS

10 skinless, boneless chicken thighs	1 medium yellow bell pepper	pepper
1 medium onion	1 tablespoon sunflower oil	whole-wheat bread and salad greens,
1 medium red bell pepper	14 ounce can chopped tomatoes	to serve
1 medium green bell pepper	2 tablespoons chopped fresh parsley	

1 Using a sharp knife, cut the chicken thighs into bite-size pieces.

2 Peel and thinly slice the onion. Halve and seed the bell peppers, and cut into small diamond shapes.

3 Heat the oil in a shallow skillet. Add the chicken and onion and fry quickly until golden brown.

4 Add the bell peppers, cook for 2–3 minutes, then stir in the tomatoes and parsley, and season with pepper.

5 Cover tightly and simmer for about 15 minutes, until the chicken and vegetables are tender. Serve hot with whole-wheat bread and salad greens.

COOK'S TIP

You can use dried parsley instead of fresh, but remember that you only need about one half of dried to fresh.

COOK'S TIP

If you are making this dish for young children, the chicken can be finely chopped or ground first.

Steamed Chicken & Spring Vegetable Packets

Serves 4

INGREDIENTS

4 boneless, skinless chicken breasts	1¾ cups young zucchini	2 teaspoons sesame oil
1 teaspoon ground lemon grass	2 stalks celery	salt and pepper
2 scallions, finely chopped	1 teaspoon light soy sauce	
1 cup young carrots	¾ cup spinach leaves	

1 With a sharp knife, make a slit through one side of each chicken breast to open out a large pocket. Sprinkle the inside of the pocket with lemon grass, salt, and pepper. Tuck the scallions into the pockets.

2 Trim the carrots, zucchini, and celery, then cut into small matchsticks. Plunge them into a pan of boiling water for 1 minute, drain, and toss in the soy sauce.

3 Pack the vegetables into the pockets in each chicken breast and fold over firmly to enclose. Reserve any remaining vegetables. Wash the spinach leaves thoroughly, then drain, and pat dry with paper towels. Wrap the chicken breasts firmly in the spinach leaves to enclose completely. If the leaves are too firm to wrap the chicken easily, steam them for a few seconds, until they are softened and flexible.

4 Place the wrapped chicken in a steamer and steam over rapidly boiling water for 20–25 minutes, depending on size.

5 Stir-fry any leftover vegetable sticks and spinach for 1–2 minutes in the sesame oil and serve with the chicken.

Chicken with Two Bell Pepper Sauce

Serves 4

INGREDIENTS

2 tablespoons olive oil	2 teaspoons tomato paste	⅔ cup dry white wine
2 medium onions, finely chopped	2 yellow bell peppers, chopped	⅔ cup chicken stock
2 garlic cloves, crushed	pinch of dried basil	bouquet garni
2 red bell peppers, chopped	4 skinless, boneless	salt and pepper
good pinch cayenne pepper	chicken breasts	fresh herbs, to garnish

1 Heat 1 tablespoon of the olive oil in each of two medium saucepans. Place half the chopped onions, 1 of the garlic cloves, the red bell peppers, the cayenne pepper, and the tomato paste in one of the saucepans. Place the remaining chopped onion, garlic, yellow bell peppers and basil in the other pan.

2 Cover each pan and cook over very low heat for 1 hour, until the bell peppers are very soft. If either mixture becomes dry, add a little water. Work each

separately in a food processor, then strain separately.

3 Return the sauces separately to each pan and season. The two sauces can be reheated while the chicken is cooking.

4 Put the chicken breasts into a skillet and add the wine and stock. Add the bouquet garni and bring the liquid to a simmer. Cook the chicken for about 20 minutes, until tender.

5 To serve, pour a pool of each sauce onto four

serving plates, slice the chicken breasts, and arrange on the plates. Garnish with fresh herbs.

COOK'S TIP

Make your own bouquet garni by tying together sprigs of your favorite herbs with string, or wrap up dried herbs in a piece of cheesecloth. A popular combination is thyme, parsley, and bay.

Chicken Risotto alla Milanese

Serves 4

INGREDIENTS

1/2 cup butter	2 1/2 cups chicken stock	1/2 cup grated Parmesan cheese,
2 pounds chicken meat, thinly sliced	2/3 cup white wine	to serve
1 large onion, chopped	1 teaspoon crumbled saffron	
2 1/2 cups risotto rice	salt and pepper	

1 Heat 4 tablespoons of the butter in a deep skillet, and fry the chicken and onion until golden brown.

2 Add the rice, stir well, and cook for 15 minutes.

3 Heat the stock until boiling and gradually add to the rice. Add the white wine, saffron, and salt and pepper to taste and mix well. Simmer over low heat for 20 minutes, stirring occasionally, and adding more stock if the risotto becomes too dry.

4 Let stand for a few minutes and just before serving, add a little more stock and simmer for a further 10 minutes. Serve the risotto, sprinkled with the grated Parmesan cheese and the remaining butter.

COOK'S TIP

A risotto should have moist, but separate grains. Stock should be added a little at a time and only when the last addition has been completely absorbed.

VARIATION

The possibilities for risotto are almost endless—try adding any of the following just at the end of cooking time: cashews and corn, lightly sautéed zucchini and basil, or artichokes and oyster mushrooms.

Elizabethan Chicken

Serves 4

INGREDIENTS

1 tablespoon butter	4 shallots, finely chopped	¹/₂ cup heavy cream
1 tablespoon sunflower oil	²/₃ cup chicken stock	1 teaspoon freshly grated nutmeg
4 skinless, boneless chicken breasts	1 tablespoon cider vinegar	cornstarch, to thicken, (optional)
	1 cup halved seedless grapes	salt and pepper

1 Heat the butter and sunflower oil in a wide, flameproof casserole or skillet and quickly fry the chicken breasts until golden brown, turning once. Remove the chicken breasts and keep warm while you are cooking the shallots.

2 Add the chopped shallots to the casserole or skillet and fry gently until softened and lightly browned. Return the chicken breasts to the pan.

3 Add the chicken stock and cider vinegar to the pan, bring to a boil, then cover, and simmer gently for 10–12 minutes, stirring occasionally.

4 Transfer the chicken to a serving dish. Add the grapes, cream, and nutmeg to the pan. Heat through, seasoning with salt and pepper to taste. Add a little cornstarch to thicken the sauce, if desired. Pour the sauce over the chicken and serve.

VARIATION

If desired, add a little dry white wine or vermouth to the sauce in step 3.

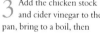

Speedy Peanut Pan-Fry

Serves 4

INGREDIENTS

2 cups zucchini

1¹/₃ cups baby corn

3³/₄ cups button mushrooms

3 cups thread egg noodles

2 tablespoons corn oil

1 tablespoon sesame oil

8 boneless chicken thighs
or 4 breasts, thinly sliced

1¹/₂ cups bean sprouts

4 tablespoons smooth
peanut butter

2 tablespoons soy sauce

2 tablespoons lime or lemon juice

¹/₂ cup roasted peanuts

pepper

cilantro, to garnish

1 Using a sharp knife, trim and thinly slice the zucchini, baby corn, and button mushrooms.

2 Bring a large pan of lightly salted water to a boil and cook the noodles for 3–4 minutes. Meanwhile, heat together the corn oil and sesame oil in a large skillet or wok. Add the chicken and fry over fairly high heat for 1 minute.

3 Add the sliced zucchini, baby corn, and button mushrooms and stir-fry for 5 minutes.

4 Add the bean sprouts, peanut butter, soy sauce, lime or lemon juice, and pepper, then cook for a further 2 minutes.

5 Drain the noodles, transfer to a serving dish, and scatter with the peanuts. Serve with the stir-fried chicken and vegetables, garnished with a sprig of fresh cilantro.

COOK'S TIP

Try serving this stir-fry with rice sticks. These are broad, pale, translucent ribbon noodles made from ground rice.

Prosciutto-Wrapped Chicken Cushions

Serves 4

INGREDIENTS

¹/₂ cup frozen spinach, thawed	2 tablespoons butter	²/₃ cup dry white or red wine
¹/₂ cup ricotta cheese	1 tablespoon olive oil	1¹/₄ cups chicken stock
pinch grated nutmeg	12 small onions or shallots	salt and pepper
4 skinless, boneless chicken breasts,	1¹/₂ cups button	carrot purée and green beans,
each weighing 6 ounces	mushrooms, sliced	to serve
4 slices prosciutto	1 tablespoon all-purpose flour	

1 Put the spinach into a strainer and press out the water with a spoon. Mix with the ricotta and nutmeg and season with salt and pepper to taste.

2 Using a sharp knife, slit each chicken breast through the side and enlarge each cut to form a pocket. Fill with the spinach mixture, reshape the chicken breasts, wrap each breast tightly in a slice of ham, and secure with toothpicks. Cover and chill in the refrigerator.

3 Heat the butter and oil in a skillet and brown the chicken breasts for 2 minutes on each side. Transfer the chicken to a large, shallow ovenproof dish and keep warm until required.

4 Fry the onions and mushrooms for 2–3 minutes, until lightly browned. Stir in the all-purpose flour, then gradually add the wine and stock. Bring to a boil, stirring constantly. Season to taste and spoon the mixture around the chicken.

5 Cook the chicken, uncovered, in a preheated oven at 400°F for 20 minutes. Turn the breasts over and cook for a further 10 minutes. Remove the toothpicks and serve with the sauce, together with carrot purée and green beans, if desired.

Poached Breast of Chicken with Whiskey Sauce

Serves 6

INGREDIENTS

2 tablespoons butter	2¹/₂ cups chicken stock	2 tablespoons freshly grated horseradish
¹/₂ cup shredded leeks	6 chicken breasts	1 teaspoon honey, warmed
¹/₃ cup diced carrot	¹/₄ cup whiskey	1 teaspoon chopped fresh parsley
¹/₄ cup diced celery	1 scant cup crème fraîche or	salt and pepper
4 shallots, sliced	sour cream	sprig of fresh parsley, to garnish

1 Melt the butter in a large saucepan and add the leeks, carrot, celery, and shallots. Cook for 3 minutes, add half the chicken stock, and cook for about 8 minutes.

2 Add the remaining chicken stock, bring to a boil, add the chicken breasts, and cook for 10 minutes.

3 Remove the chicken and thinly slice. Place on a large, hot serving dish and keep warm until required.

4 In another saucepan, heat the whiskey until reduced by half. Strain the chicken stock through a fine strainer, add to the pan, and reduce the liquid by half.

5 Add the crème fraîche or sour cream, the horseradish and the honey. Heat gently and add the chopped parsley and salt and pepper to taste. Stir well.

6 Pour a little of the whiskey sauce around the chicken and pour the remaining sauce into a sauceboat to serve.

7 Serve with a vegetable patty made from the leftover vegetables, mashed potato, and fresh vegetables. Garnish with the parsley sprig.

Deviled Chicken

Serves 2-3

INGREDIENTS

¹/₄ cup all-purpose flour
1 tablespoon cayenne pepper
1 teaspoon paprika
12 ounces skinless, boneless
    chicken, diced

2 tablespoons butter
1 onion, finely chopped
scant 2 cups milk, warmed
4 tablespoons apple purée

³/₄ cup white grapes
²/₃ cup sour cream
sprinkle of paprika, to garnish

1 Mix the flour, cayenne pepper, and paprika together and use to coat the chicken.

2 Shake off any excess flour. Melt the butter in a saucepan and gently fry the chicken with the onion for 4 minutes.

3 Stir in the flour and spice mixture. Add the milk slowly, stirring until the sauce thickens.

4 Simmer until the sauce is smooth.

5 Add the apple purée and grapes and simmer gently for 20 minutes.

6 Transfer the chicken and deviled sauce to a serving dish and top with sour cream and a sprinkle of paprika.

VARIATION

For a healthier alternative to the sour cream in this recipe, use unsweetened yogurt.

COOK'S TIP

Add more paprika if desired—as it is quite a mild spice, you can add plenty without it being too overpowering.

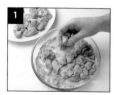

Italian Chicken Spirals

Serves 4

INGREDIENTS

4 skinless, boneless, chicken breasts	2 cups whole wheat	1 tablespoon lemon juice
1 cup fresh basil leaves	pasta spirals	1 tablespoon olive oil
2 tablespoons hazelnuts	2 sun-dried tomatoes	1 tablespoon capers
1 garlic clove, crushed	or fresh tomatoes	1/2 cup black olives
		salt and pepper

1 Beat the chicken breasts with a rolling pin to flatten evenly.

2 Place the basil and hazelnuts in a food processor and process until finely chopped. Mix with the garlic, salt, and pepper.

3 Spread the basil mixture over the chicken breasts and roll up from one short end to enclose the filling. Wrap the chicken rolls tightly in foil so that they hold their shape, then seal the ends well.

4 Bring a large pan of lightly salted water to boil and cook the pasta until tender, but still firm to the bite.

5 Place the chicken parcels in a steamer basket or colander set over the pan, cover tightly, and steam for 10 minutes. Meanwhile, dice the tomatoes.

6 Drain the pasta and return to the pan with the lemon juice, olive oil, tomatoes, capers, and olives. Heat through.

7 Pierce the chicken with a a sharp knife to make sure that the juices run clear and not pink, then slice the chicken, arrange it over the pasta, and serve.

VARIATION

Sun-dried tomatoes have a wonderful, rich flavor, but if you can't find them, use fresh tomatoes.

Garlic Chicken Cushions

Serves 4

INGREDIENTS

4 partially-boned chicken breasts	1 tablespoon olive oil	6 tablespoons wine or chicken stock
¹/₂ cup frozen spinach, thawed	1 onion, chopped	10 stuffed olives, sliced
¹/₂ cup ricotta cheese	1 red bell pepper, sliced	salt and pepper
2 garlic cloves, crushed	14 ounce can chopped tomatoes	pasta, to serve

1 Make a slit between the skin and meat on one side of each chicken breast. Lift the skin to form a pocket, being careful to leave the skin attached to the other side.

2 Put the spinach into a strainer and press out the water with a spoon. Mix with the ricotta, half the garlic, and seasoning.

3 Spoon the spinach and ricotta mixture under the skin of each chicken breast, then secure the edge of the skin with toothpicks.

4 Heat the oil in a skillet, add the onion, and fry for a minute, stirring. Add the remaining garlic and red bell pepper and cook for 2 minutes. Stir in the tomatoes, wine or stock, olives, and seasoning. Set the sauce aside and chill the chicken if preparing in advance.

5 Bring the sauce to a boil, pour into a shallow ovenproof dish, and arrange the chicken breasts on top in a single layer.

6 Cook, uncovered, in a preheated oven at 400°F for 35 minutes, until the chicken is golden and cooked through. Test by making a slit in one of the chicken breasts with a sharp knife to make sure the juices run clear and not pink. Spoon a little of the sauce over the chicken breasts then transfer to warm individual serving plates. Serve with pasta.

Chicken Strips & Dips

Serves 2

INGREDIENTS

2 boneless chicken breasts	PEANUT DIP:	TOMATO DIP:
2 tablespoons all-purpose flour	3 tablespoons smooth or crunchy	5 tablespoons ricotta cheese
1 tablespoon sunflower oil	peanut butter	1 medium tomato
	4 tablespoons unsweetened yogurt	2 teaspoons tomato paste
	1 teaspoon grated orange rind	1 teaspoon chopped fresh chives
	orange juice (optional)	

1 Using a sharp knife, slice the chicken into fairly thin strips and toss in the flour to coat.

2 Heat the oil in a nonstick skillet and fry the chicken until golden and thoroughly cooked. Remove the chicken strips from the pan and drain well on absorbent paper towels.

3 To make the peanut dip, mix together all the ingredients in a bowl (if desired, add a little orange juice to thin the dip).

4 To make the tomato dip, chop the tomato and mix with the remaining ingredients.

5 Serve the chicken strips with the dips and a selection of vegetable sticks for dipping.

VARIATION

For a lower-fat alternative, poach the strips of chicken in a small amount of boiling chicken stock for 6–8 minutes.

VARIATION

For a refreshing guacamole dip, combine 1 mashed avocado, 2 finely chopped scallions, 1 chopped tomato, 1 crushed garlic clove, and a squeeze of lemon juice. Remember to add the lemon juice immediately after the avocado has been mashed to prevent discoloration.

Chicken Lady Jayne

Serves 4

INGREDIENTS

4 chicken breasts, each about 4½ ounces	rind and juice of 1 lemon	3 tablespoons coffee liqueur
4 tablespoons corn oil	2 teaspoons Worcestershire sauce	3 tablespoons brandy, warmed
8 shallots, sliced	4 tablespoons chicken stock	
	1 tablespoon chopped fresh parsley	

1 Place the chicken breasts on a chopping board, cover with plastic wrap and pound them until evenly flattened with a wooden meat mallet or a rolling pin.

2 Heat the oil in a large skillet and fry the chicken for 3 minutes on each side. Add the shallots and cook for a further 3 minutes.

3 Sprinkle with lemon juice and lemon rind and add the Worcestershire sauce and chicken stock. Cook for 2 minutes, then sprinkle with the chopped fresh parsley.

4 Add the coffee liqueur and the brandy and flame the chicken by lighting the spirit with a taper or long match. Cook until the flame is extinguished and serve.

COOK'S TIP

Instead of chicken breasts, suprêmes can also be used. A suprême is a chicken fillet that sometimes has part of the wing bone remaining.

COOK'S TIP

Flattening the breasts means that they take less time to cook.

Golden Glazed Chicken

Serves 6

INGREDIENTS

6 boneless chicken breasts	2 tablespoons clear honey	3 tablespoons chopped mint
1 teaspoon turmeric	2 tablespoons sunflower oil	salt and pepper
1 tablespoon wholegrain mustard	1³/4 cups long grain rice	mint sprigs, to garnish
1¹/4 cups orange juice	1 orange	

1 With a sharp knife, mark the surface of the chicken breasts in a diamond pattern. Mix together the turmeric, mustard, orange juice, and honey and pour over the chicken. Chill until required.

2 Lift the chicken from the marinade and pat dry on paper towels.

3 Heat the oil in a wide pan, add the chicken, and sauté until golden, turning once. Drain off any excess oil. Pour the marinade over it, cover, and simmer for 10–15 minutes, until the chicken is tender.

4 Boil the rice in lightly salted water until tender, and drain well. Finely grate the rind from the orange and stir it into the rice with the mint.

5 Using a sharp knife, remove the peel and white pith from the orange and cut the flesh into segments.

6 Serve the chicken with the orange and mint rice, garnished with orange segments and mint sprigs.

VARIATION

To make a slightly sharper sauce, use small grapefruit instead of the oranges.

Mediterranean Chicken Packets

Serves 6

INGREDIENTS

1 tablespoon olive oil	3½ cups sliced zucchini	pepper
6 skinless chicken breast fillets	6 large tomatoes, sliced	rice or pasta, to serve
2 cups Mozzarella cheese	1 small bunch fresh basil or oregano	

1 Cut six pieces of foil each about 10 inches square. Brush the foil squares lightly with oil and set aside until required.

2 With a sharp knife, slash each chicken breast at intervals, then slice the Mozzarella cheese and place between the cuts in the chicken.

3 Divide the zucchini and tomatoes between the pieces of foil and sprinkle with black pepper. Tear or roughly chop the basil or oregano leaves and scatter them over the vegetables in each foil packet.

4 Place the chicken on top of each pile of vegetables, then wrap in the foil to enclose the chicken and vegetables, tucking in the ends.

5 Place the foil packets on a cookie sheet and bake in a preheated oven at 400°F for about 30 minutes.

6 To serve, unwrap each foil packet and serve with rice or pasta.

COOK'S TIP

To aid cooking, place the vegetables and chicken on the shiny side of the foil so that once the packet is wrapped up, the dull surface of the foil is facing outward. This ensures that the heat is absorbed into the packet and not reflected away from it.

Chicken, Corn, & Snow Pea Sauté

Serves 4

INGREDIENTS

4 skinless, boneless
   chicken breasts
1⅓ cups baby corn
9 ounces snow peas

2 tablespoons sunflower oil
1 tablespoon sherry vinegar
1 tablespoon clear honey
1 tablespoon light soy sauce

1 tablespoon sunflower seeds
pepper
rice or egg noodles, to serve

1 Using a sharp knife, slice the chicken breasts into long, thin strips. Cut the baby corn in half lengthwise and top and tail the snow peas. Set the prepared vegetables aside until they are required.

2 Heat the sunflower oil in a wok or a wide skillet. Add the chicken and fry over fairly high heat, stirring constantly, for 1 minute.

3 Add the corn and snow peas and stir over moderate heat for 5–8 minutes, until evenly cooked through.

4 Mix together the sherry vinegar, honey, and soy sauce and stir into the pan with the sunflower seeds. Season with pepper to taste. Cook, stirring constantly, for 1 minute. Serve the sauté hot with rice or Chinese egg noodles.

COOK'S TIP

Rice vinegar or balsamic vinegar would make a good substitute for the sherry vinegar.

Savory Chicken Sausages

Serves 4–6

INGREDIENTS

13 cups fresh bread crumbs

9 ounces cooked chicken, ground

1 small leek, finely chopped

pinch of mixed herbs

pinch of mustard powder

2 eggs, separated

4 tablespoons milk

crisp bread crumbs, for coating

2 tablespoons beef drippings

salt and pepper

1 In a large mixing bowl, combine the bread crumbs, ground chicken, leek, mixed herbs, and mustard powder, and season with salt and pepper. Mix together until thoroughly incorporated.

2 Add 1 whole egg and an egg yolk with a little milk to bind the mixture.

3 Divide the mixture into 6 or 8 and shape into thick or thin sausages.

4 Whisk the remaining egg white until frothy. Coat the sausages first in the egg white, and then in the crisp bread crumbs.

5 Heat the drippings and fry the sausages for 6 minutes, until golden brown. Serve at once.

VARIATION

If you want to lower the saturated fat content of this recipe, use a little oil for frying instead of the drippings.

COOK'S TIP

Make your own ground chicken by working lean cuts of chicken in a food processor.

Golden Chicken Risotto

Serves 4

INGREDIENTS

2 tablespoons sunflower oil
1 tablespoon butter or margarine
1 medium leek, thinly sliced
1 large yellow bell pepper, diced

3 skinless, boneless chicken
breasts, diced
12 ounces risotto rice
few strands saffron

6 1/4 cups chicken stock
7 ounce can corn
1/2 cup toasted unsalted peanuts
1/2 cup grated Parmesan cheese
salt and pepper

1 Heat the oil and butter or margarine in a large saucepan. Fry the leek and bell pepper for 1 minute, then stir in the chicken, and cook, stirring until golden brown.

2 Stir in the rice and cook for 2–3 minutes.

3 Stir in the saffron strands and salt and pepper to taste. Add the stock, a little at a time, cover, and cook over low heat, stirring occasionally, for about 20 minutes, until the rice is tender and most of the liquid has been absorbed. Do not let the risotto dry out—add more stock if necessary.

4 Stir in the corn, peanuts, and Parmesan cheese, then adjust the seasoning to taste. Serve the risotto hot.

COOK'S TIP

Risottos can be frozen, before adding the Parmesan cheese, for up to 1 month, but remember to reheat this risotto thoroughly as it contains chicken.

Quick Chicken Bake

Serves 4

INGREDIENTS

1 pound 2 ounces ground chicken	1¼ cups chicken stock	¾ cup grated semihard white cheese
1 large onion, finely chopped	pinch of fresh thyme	salt and pepper
2 carrots, finely diced	2 pounds potatoes, creamed with	peas, to serve
2 tablespoons all-purpose flour	butter and milk and highly	
1 tablespoon tomato paste	seasoned	

1 Brown the ground chicken, onion, and carrots in a nonstick saucepan for 5 minutes, stirring frequently.

2 Sprinkle the chicken with the flour and simmer for a further 2 minutes.

3 Gradually blend in the tomato paste and stock, then simmer for 15 minutes. Season and add the thyme.

4 Transfer the chicken and vegetable mixture to an ovenproof casserole and set aside to cool.

5 Spoon the mashed potato over the chicken mixture and sprinkle with the cheese. Bake in a preheated oven at 400°F for 20 minutes, or until the cheese is bubbling and golden, then serve, straight from the casserole, with the peas.

VARIATION

Instead of plain cheese, you could sprinkle a flavored cheese over the top. There are a variety of cheeses blended with onion and chives, and these are ideal for melting as a topping. Alternatively, you could use a mixture of cheeses, depending on whatever you have at hand.

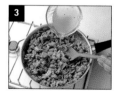

Tom's Toad in the Hole

Serves 4–6

INGREDIENTS

1 cup plain all-purpose flour	1 scant cup milk	9 ounces chicken breasts
pinch of salt	1/3 cup water	9 ounces Cumberland sausage
1 egg, beaten	2 tablespoons beef drippings	

1 Mix the flour and salt in a bowl, make a well in the center, and add the beaten egg.

2 Add half the milk, and using a wooden spoon, gradually work in the flour.

3 Beat the mixture until smooth, then add the remaining milk and water.

4 Beat again until the mixture is smooth. Set the mixture aside to stand for at least 1 hour. Add the drippings to individual baking pans or to one large baking pan.

5 Cut up the chicken and sausage so that you have a generous piece in each individual pan or several scattered around the large pan.

6 Heat the pans in a preheated oven at 425°F for 5 minutes, until very hot. Remove the pans from the oven and pour in the batter, leaving space for the mixture to expand.

7 Return to the oven to cook for 35 minutes, until risen and golden brown. While cooking, do not open the oven door for at least 30 minutes.

8 Serve hot, with chicken or onion gravy, or alone.

VARIATION

Use skinless, boneless chicken legs, instead of chicken breast, in the recipe. Cut up as directed. Instead of Cumberland sausage, use your favorite variety of sausage.

Neapolitan Porkchops

Serves 4

INGREDIENTS

2 tbsp olive oil	2 tsp yeast extract	2 tbsp fresh basil, shredded
1 garlic clove, chopped	4 pork loin chops, each about	freshly grated Parmesan cheese,
1 large onion, sliced	4¹/₂ oz	to serve
14 ounce can tomatoes	³/₄ cup pitted black olives	

1 Heat the oil in a large skillet. Add the onions and garlic and sauté for 3–4 minutes, or until the onions are just beginning to soften.

2 Add the tomatoes and yeast extract to the skillet and simmer for about 5 minutes, or until the sauce just starts to thicken.

3 Cook the porkchops under a preheated broiler for 5 minutes on both sides, until the the meat is golden and cooked through. Set the porkchops aside and keep warm.

4 Add the olives and fresh shredded basil to the sauce in the skillet and stir quickly to combine.

5 Transfer the chops to warm serving plates. Top with the sauce, sprinkle with freshly grated Parmesan cheese, and serve immediately.

COOK'S TIP

Parmesan is a mature and exceptionally hard cheese produced in Italy. You need to add only a little, as it has a very strong flavor.

COOK'S TIP

There are many types of canned tomato available – for example plum tomatoes, or chopped tomatoes in water, or chopped sieved tomatoes (passata). The chopped variety are often canned with added flavors, such as garlic, basil, onion, chili, and mixed herbs, and are a good standby.

Escalopes with Italian Sausage & Capers

Serves 4

INGREDIENTS

1 tbsp olive oil	finely grated rind and juice of	4 turkey or veal escalopes, each
6 canned anchovy fillets, drained	1 orange	about 4^{1}/$_{2}$ oz
1 tbsp capers, drained	^{3}/$_{4}$ cup diced Italian sausage	salt and pepper
1 tbsp fresh rosemary, stalks removed	3 tomatoes, skinned and chopped	crusty bread or cooked polenta,
		to serve

1 Heat the oil in a large skillet. Add the anchovies, capers, fresh rosemary, orange rind and juice, Italian sausage, and tomatoes and cook for about 5–6 minutes, stirring occasionally.

2 Meanwhile, place the turkey or veal escalopes between sheets of wax paper. Pound the meat with a meat mallet or the end of a rolling pin to flatten it.

3 Add the meat to the mixture in the skillet. Season to taste with salt and pepper, cover, and cook for 3–5 minutes on each side, or slightly longer if the meat is thicker.

4 Transfer to serving plates and serve with fresh crusty bread or cooked polenta.

COOK'S TIP

Polenta is typical of northern Italian cuisine. It is often fried or toasted and used to mop up the juices of the main course.

VARIATION

Try using 4-minute steaks, slightly flattened, instead of the turkey or veal. Cook them for 4–5 minutes on top of the sauce in the skillet.

Creamed Strips of Sirloin with Rigatoni

Serves 4

INGREDIENTS

6 tbsp butter	2 tbsp dry sherry	PASTA:
1 pound sirloin steak, trimmed	⅝ cup heavy cream	1 pound dried rigatoni
and cut into thin strips	salt and pepper	2 tbsp olive oil
6 ounces button mushrooms,	4 slices hot toast, cut into	2 fresh basil sprigs
sliced	triangles, to serve	8 tbsp butter
1 tsp mustard		
pinch of freshly grated ginger		
root		

1 Preheat the oven to 375°F. Melt the butter in a large skillet and gently fry the steak, stirring frequently, for 6 minutes. Transfer to an ovenproof dish and keep warm.

2 Add the mushrooms to the remaining juices in the skillet and cook for 2–3 minutes. Add the mustard, ginger, and salt and pepper to taste. Cook

for about 2 minutes, then add the sherry and cream. Cook for an additional 3 minutes, then pour the cream sauce over the steak.

3 Bake the steak and cream mixture in the preheated oven for 10 minutes.

4 Bring a large saucepan of lightly salted water to a boil. Add the rigatoni,

olive oil, and 1 basil sprig and boil rapidly for 10 minutes, until tender but still firm to the bite. Drain the pasta and transfer to a warm serving plate. Toss the pasta with the butter and garnish with the remaining basil sprig.

5 Serve the steak with the pasta and triangles of warm toast. Serve the rigatoni separately.

Egg Noodles with Beef

Serves 4

INGREDIENTS

10 ounces egg noodles
3 tbsp walnut oil
1-inch piece fresh ginger root,
    cut into thin strips
5 scallions, finely shredded
2 garlic cloves, finely chopped
1 red bell pepper, cored,
    seeded, and thinly sliced

3½ ounces button
    mushrooms, thinly sliced
12 ounces fillet steak, cut into
    thin strips
1 tbsp cornstarch
5 tbsp dry sherry
3 tbsp soy sauce
1 tsp soft brown sugar

1 cup bean sprouts
1 tbsp sesame oil
salt and pepper
scallion strips, to garnish

1 Bring a large pan of water to a boil. Add the noodles and cook according to the instructions on the packet. Drain the noodles, set aside, and keep warm.

2 Heat the walnut oil in a preheated wok and stir-fry the ginger, scallions, and garlic for 45 seconds. Add the bell pepper, mushrooms, and steak and stir-fry for 4 minutes. Season to taste.

3 Mix together the cornstarch, sherry, and soy sauce in a small bowl to form a paste, and pour into the wok. Sprinkle in the brown sugar and stir-fry all of the ingredients for 2 minutes longer.

4 Add the bean sprouts, drained noodles, and sesame oil to the wok, stir and toss together for 1 minute. Transfer to serving plates, garnish with strips of scallion and serve.

COOK'S TIP

If you do not have a wok, you could prepare this dish in a skillet. However, a wok is preferable, as the round base ensures an even distribution of heat and it is easier to keep stirring and tossing the contents when stir-frying.

Stir-Fried Pork with Pasta & Vegetables

Serves 4

INGREDIENTS

3 tbsp sesame oil
12 ounces pork tenderloin, cut into thin strips
1 pound dried taglioni
1 tbsp olive oil
8 shallots, sliced
2 garlic cloves, finely chopped
1-inch piece fresh ginger root, grated

1 fresh green chili, finely chopped
1 red bell pepper, cored, seeded, and thinly sliced
1 green bell pepper, cored, seeded, and thinly sliced
3 zucchini, thinly sliced
2 tbsp ground almonds
1 tsp ground cinnamon

1 tbsp oyster sauce
2 ounces creamed coconut (see Cook's Tip), grated
salt and pepper

1 Heat the sesame oil in a preheated wok. Season the pork and stir-fry for 5 minutes.

2 Bring a pan of salted water to a boil. Add the taglioni and olive oil and cook for 12 minutes. Set aside and keep warm.

3 Add the shallots, garlic, ginger, and chili to the wok and stir-fry for 2 minutes. Add the bell peppers and zucchini and stir-fry for 1 minute.

4 Finally, add the ground almonds, cinnamon, oyster sauce, and creamed coconut to the wok and stir-fry for 1 minute.

5 Drain the taglioni and transfer to a serving dish. Top with the stir-fry and serve immediately.

COOK'S TIP

Creamed coconut is available from Chinese and Asian food stores and some large supermarkets. It is sold in compressed blocks and adds a concentrated coconut flavor to the dish.

Orecchiette with Pork in Cream Sauce, Garnished with Quail Eggs

Serves 4

INGREDIENTS

1 pound pork tenderloin, thinly sliced	$^7/_8$ cup Italian red wine sauce	12 quail eggs (see Cook's Tip)
4 tbsp olive oil	1 tbsp lemon juice	salt
8 ounces button mushrooms, sliced	pinch of saffron	
	3 cups dried orecchiette	
	4 tbsp heavy cream	

1 Pound the slices of pork until wafer thin, then cut into strips.

2 Heat the olive oil in a skillet and stir-fry the pork for 5 minutes, then stir-fry the mushrooms for a further 2 minutes.

3 Pour in the Italian red wine sauce, then simmer for 20 minutes.

4 Meanwhile, bring a large saucepan of lightly salted water to a boil. Add the lemon juice, saffron, and orecchiette and cook for 12 minutes, until tender but still firm to the bite. Drain the pasta and keep warm.

5 Stir the cream into the pan with the pork and heat gently for 3 minutes.

6 Boil the quail eggs for 3 minutes, cool them in cold water, and remove the shells.

7 Transfer the pasta to a warm serving plate, top with the pork and sauce, and garnish with the eggs. Serve immediately.

COOK'S TIP

In this recipe, the quail eggs are soft-cooked. As they are very difficult to shell when warm, they should be thoroughly cooled first. Otherwise, they will break up unattractively.

Sliced Breast of Duckling
with Linguine

Serves 4

INGREDIENTS

4 10¹/₂-ounce boned breasts
   of duckling
2 tbsp butter
³/₈ cup finely chopped carrots
4 tbsp finely chopped shallots
1 tbsp lemon juice
⁵/₈ cup meat stock
4 tbsp clear honey

³/₄ cup fresh or thawed
   frozen raspberries
¹/₄ cup all-purpose flour
1 tbsp Worcestershire sauce
14 ounces fresh linguine
1 tbsp olive oil
salt and pepper

TO GARNISH:
fresh raspberries
fresh sprigs of parsley

1 Trim and score the duck breasts and season well. Melt the butter in a skillet and fry the duck breasts until lightly colored.

2 Add the carrots, shallots, lemon juice, and half the meat stock and simmer for 1 minute. Stir in half the honey and half the raspberries. Sprinkle in half the flour and cook, stirring constantly, for 3 minutes. Add pepper and the Worcestershire sauce.

3 Stir in the remaining stock and cook for 1 minute. Stir in the remaining honey, raspberries, and flour. Cook for 3 minutes longer.

4 Remove the duck from the pan, but continue simmering the sauce.

5 Bring a large pan of salted water to a boil. Add the linguine and olive oil and cook until tender. Drain and divide between 4 individual plates.

6 Slice the duck breasts lengthwise into ¹/₄-inch thick pieces. Pour a little sauce over the pasta and arrange the sliced duck in a fan shape on top of it. Garnish and serve.

Chili Chicken

Serves 4

INGREDIENTS

12 ounces skinless, boneless
   lean chicken
1/2 tsp salt
1 egg white, lightly beaten
2 tbsp cornstarch
4 tbsp vegetable oil

2 garlic cloves, crushed
1/2-inch piece fresh ginger
   root, grated
1 red bell pepper, seeded and diced
1 green bell pepper, seeded
   and diced

2 fresh red chilies, chopped
2 tbsp light soy sauce
1 tbsp dry sherry or Chinese rice
   wine
1 tbsp wine vinegar

1 Cut the chicken into cubes and place in a mixing bowl. Add the salt, egg white, cornstarch, and 1 tablespoon of the oil. Turn the chicken in the mixture to coat thoroughly.

2 Heat the remaining oil in a preheated wok. Add the garlic and ginger and stir-fry for 30 seconds.

3 Add the chicken pieces to the wok and stir-fry for 2–3 minutes, or until browned.

4 Stir in the bell peppers, chilies, soy sauce, sherry or Chinese rice wine, and wine vinegar and cook for a further 2–3 minutes, until the chicken is cooked through. Transfer to a warm serving dish and serve.

VARIATION

This recipe works well if you use 12 ounces lean steak, cut into thin strips, or 1 pound raw shrimp, instead of the chicken.

COOK'S TIP

When preparing chilies, wear protective gloves to prevent the juices from burning and irritating your hands. Be careful not to touch your face, especially your lips or eyes, until you have washed your hands.

Lemon Chicken

Serves 4

INGREDIENTS

vegetable oil, for deep-frying
1½ pounds skinless, boneless
  chicken, cut into strips
lemon slices and shredded scallion,
  to garnish

SAUCE:
1 tbsp cornstarch
6 tbsp cold water
3 tbsp fresh lemon juice

2 tbsp sweet sherry
½ tsp superfine sugar

1 Heat the oil in a preheated wok until almost smoking. Reduce the heat and stir-fry the chicken strips for 3–4 minutes, until cooked through. Remove the chicken with a slotted spoon, set aside, and keep warm. Drain the oil from the wok.

2 To make the sauce, mix the cornstarch with 2 tablespoons of the water to form a paste.

3 Pour the lemon juice and remaining water

into the wok. Add the sherry and sugar and bring to a boil, stirring until the sugar has completely dissolved.

4 Stir in the cornstarch mixture and return to a boil. Reduce the heat and simmer, stirring constantly, for about 2-3 minutes, until the sauce is thickened and becomes clear.

5 Transfer the chicken strips to a warm serving plate and pour the lemon sauce over the top. Garnish with the lemon slices and

shredded scallion and serve immediately.

COOK'S TIP

If you would prefer to use chicken portions rather than strips, cook them in the oil, covered, over a low heat for about 30 minutes, or until cooked through.

Chicken Chop Suey

Serves 4

INGREDIENTS

4 tbsp light soy sauce
2 tsp light brown sugar
1¼ pounds skinless, boneless
    chicken breasts

3 tbsp vegetable oil
2 onions, quartered
2 garlic cloves, crushed
12 ounces bean sprouts
1 tbsp sesame oil

1 tbsp cornstarch
3 tbsp water
2 cups chicken stock
shredded leek, to garnish

1 Mix the soy sauce and sugar together, stirring until the sugar has dissolved.

2 Trim any fat from the chicken and cut the meat into thin strips. Place the chicken strips in a shallow glass dish and spoon the soy mixture over them, turning to coat. Marinate in the refrigerator for 20 minutes.

3 Heat the oil in a preheated wok. Add the chicken and stir-fry for 2–3 minutes, until golden brown.

4 Add the onions and garlic and cook for a further 2 minutes. Add the bean sprouts, cook for a further 4–5 minutes, then add the sesame oil.

5 Blend the cornstarch with the water to form a smooth paste. Pour the chicken stock into the wok, together with the cornstarch paste, and bring the mixture to a boil, stirring constantly until the sauce is thickened and clear. Transfer to a warm serving dish, garnish with shredded leek, and serve immediately.

VARIATION

This recipe may be made with strips of lean steak, pork, or with mixed vegetables. Change the type of stock accordingly.

Spicy Peanut Chicken

Serves 4

INGREDIENTS

10¹/₂ ounces skinless, boneless
    chicken breast
2 tbsp peanut oil
1 cup unsalted peanuts
1 fresh red chili, sliced
1 green bell pepper, seeded and cut
    into strips

1 tsp sesame oil
fried rice, to serve

SAUCE:
²/₃ cup chicken stock
1 tbsp Chinese rice wine or
    dry sherry

1 tbsp light soy sauce
1¹/₂ tsp light brown sugar
2 garlic cloves, crushed
1 tsp grated fresh ginger root
1 tsp rice wine vinegar

1 Trim any fat from the chicken and cut the meat into 1-inch cubes.

2 Heat the peanut oil i n a preheated wok. Add the peanuts and stir-fry for 1 minute. Remove the peanuts with a slotted spoon and set aside.

3 Add the chicken to the wok and cook for 1–2 minutes. Stir in the chili and green bell pepper and cook for 1 minute. Remove

from the wok with a slotted spoon and set aside.

4 Put half the peanuts in a food processor and process until almost smooth. Alternatively, place them in a plastic bag and crush them with a rolling pin.

5 To make the sauce, add the chicken stock, Chinese rice wine or dry sherry, soy sauce, sugar, garlic, ginger, and rice wine vinegar to the wok.

6 Heat the sauce gently and stir in the peanut purée, peanuts, chicken, chili, and bell pepper.

7 Sprinkle the sesame oil into the wok, stir, and cook for 1 minute. Serve hot with fried rice.

Chinese Chicken Salad

Serves 4

INGREDIENTS

8 ounces skinless, boneless chicken breasts	1 red bell pepper, seeded and thinly sliced	sauce:
2 tsp light soy sauce	1 carrot, peeled and cut into matchsticks	2 tsp rice wine vinegar
1 tsp sesame oil		1 tbsp light soy sauce
1 tsp sesame seeds	3 baby corncobs, sliced	dash of chili oil
2 tbsp vegetable oil	chives and carrot matchsticks, to	
4¹/₂ ounces bean sprouts	garnish	

1 Place the chicken in a shallow glass dish.

2 Mix together the soy sauce and sesame oil and pour the mixture over the chicken. Sprinkle with sesame seeds and let stand for 20 minutes.

3 Remove the chicken from the marinade and cut the meat into slices.

4 Heat the oil in a pre-heated wok. Add the chicken and fry for 4-5 minutes, until cooked through and golden brown on both sides. Remove the chicken from the wok with a slotted spoon, set aside, and let cool.

5 Add the bean sprouts, bell pepper, carrot, and baby corncobs to the wok and stir-fry for 2–3 minutes. Remove from the wok with a slotted spoon and cool.

6 To make the sauce, mix the rice wine vinegar, light soy sauce, and chili oil together.

7 Arrange the chicken and vegetables on a serving plate. Spoon the sauce over the salad, garnish with snipped chives and carrot matchsticks, and serve.

COOK'S TIP

If you have time, make the sauce and let stand for 30 minutes for the flavors to fully develop.

Honey-Glazed Duck

Serves 4

INGREDIENTS

1 tsp dark soy sauce
2 tbsp clear honey
1 tsp garlic vinegar
2 garlic cloves, crushed
1 tsp ground star anise

2 tsp cornstarch
2 tsp water

2 large boneless duck breasts, about
8 ounces each

celery leaves, cucumber
matchsticks, and snipped
chives, to garnish

1 Mix together the soy sauce, clear honey, garlic vinegar, garlic, and star anise. Blend the cornstarch with the water to form a smooth paste and stir it into the mixture.

2 Place the duck breasts in a shallow ovenproof dish. Brush with the soy marinade, turning to coat them completely. Cover and marinate in the refrigerator for at least 2 hours, or overnight if possible.

3 Remove the duck from the marinade and cook in a preheated oven at 425°F for 20–25 minutes, basting frequently with the glaze.

4 Remove the duck from the oven and transfer to a preheated broiler. Broil for about 3–4 minutes to caramelize the top of the duck.

5 Remove the duck from the broiler pan and cut into thin slices. Arrange the duck slices in a warm serving dish, garnish with celery leaves, cucumber matchsticks, and snipped chives, and serve immediately.

COOK'S TIP

If the duck begins to burn slightly while it is cooking in the oven, cover with foil. To be sure the duck breasts are cooked through, insert the point of a sharp knife into the thickest part of the flesh. The juices should run clear.

Pork Fry with Vegetables

Serves 4

INGREDIENTS

12 ounces lean pork tenderloin
2 tbsp vegetable oil
2 garlic cloves, crushed
$\frac{1}{2}$-inch piece fresh ginger root, cut into slivers
1 red bell pepper, seeded and diced

1 carrot, peeled and cut into thin strips
1 fennel bulb, sliced
1 ounce canned water chestnuts, drained and halved
$2\frac{3}{4}$ ounces bean sprouts

2 tbsp Chinese rice wine
$1\frac{1}{4}$ cups pork or chicken stock
pinch of dark brown sugar
1 tsp cornstarch
2 tsp water

1 Cut the pork into thin slices. Heat the oil in a preheated wok. Add the garlic, ginger, and pork and stir-fry for 1–2 minutes, until the meat is sealed.

2 Add the bell pepper, carrot, fennel, and water chestnuts to the wok and stir-fry for about 2-3 minutes.

3 Add the bean sprouts and stir-fry for 1 minute. Remove the pork and vegetables from the wok.

4 Add the Chinese rice wine, pork or chicken stock, and sugar to the wok. Blend the cornstarch to a smooth paste with the water and stir it into the sauce. Bring to a boil, stirring constantly until thickened and clear.

5 Return the meat and vegetables to the wok and cook for 1–2 minutes, until thoroughly heated through and well coated with the sauce. Transfer to a warm serving dish and serve.

COOK'S TIP

Use dry sherry instead of the Chinese rice wine if you have difficulty obtaining it.

Beef & Broccoli Stir-Fry

Serves 4

INGREDIENTS

8 ounces lean steak, trimmed
2 garlic cloves, crushed
dash of chili oil
1/2-inch piece fresh ginger
 root, grated

1/2 tsp Chinese five-spice powder
2 tbsp dark soy sauce
2 tbsp vegetable oil
5 ounces broccoli florets
1 tbsp light soy sauce

2/3 cup beef stock
2 tsp cornstarch
4 tsp water
carrot strips, to garnish

1 Cut the steak into thin strips and place in a shallow glass dish. Mix together the garlic, chili oil, grated ginger, Chinese five-spice powder, and soy sauce in a small bowl and pour the mixture over the beef, tossing to coat the strips evenly. Marinate for 30 minutes.

2 Heat 1 tablespoon of the oil in a preheated wok. Add the broccoli and stir-fry over a medium heat for 4–5 minutes. Remove from the wok with a slotted spoon and set aside.

3 Heat the remaining vegetable oil in the wok. Add the steak strips, together with the marinade, and stir-fry for about 2-3 minutes, until the steak is browned all over and sealed.

4 Return the broccoli to the wok and stir in the soy sauce and stock.

5 Blend the cornstarch with the water to form a smooth paste and stir it into the wok. Bring to a boil, stirring until thickened and clear. Cook for 1 minute.

6 Transfer the beef and broccoli stir-fry to a warm serving dish, arrange the carrot strips in a lattice pattern on top, and serve immediately.

COOK'S TIP

Marinate the steak for several hours for a fuller flavor. Cover and marinate in the refrigerator if preparing in advance.

Spicy Beef

Serves 4

INGREDIENTS

8 ounces fillet steak
2 garlic cloves, crushed
1 tsp powdered star anise
1 tbsp dark soy sauce
scallion tassels, to garnish (optional)

SAUCE:
2 tbsp vegetable oil
1 bunch scallions, halved
        lengthwise
1 tbsp dark soy sauce

1 tbsp dry sherry
1/4 tsp chili sauce
2/3 cup water
2 tsp cornstarch
4 tsp water

1 Cut the steak into thin strips and place in a shallow dish.

2 Mix together the garlic, star anise, and dark soy sauce in a bowl and pour the mixture over the steak strips, turning them to ensure that they are thoroughly coated. Cover with plastic wrap and marinate in the refrigerator for at least 1 hour, preferably overnight.

3 Heat the oil in a preheated wok. Reduce the heat slightly, add the halved scallions and stir-fry for 1-2 minutes. Remove from the wok with a slotted spoon and set aside.

4 Add the beef to the wok, together with the marinade, and stir-fry for 3-4 minutes. Return the halved scallions to the wok and add the soy sauce, sherry, chili sauce and the water.

5 Blend the cornstarch to a paste with the 4 tsp water and stir into the wok. Bring to a boil, stirring until the sauce thickens and clears.

6 Transfer to a warm serving dish, garnish with scallion tassels, if using, and serve immediately.

COOK'S TIP

Omit the chili sauce for a milder dish.

Beef & Beans

Serves 4

INGREDIENTS

1 pound fillet steak, cut into
   1-inch pieces

MARINADE:
2 tsp cornstarch
2 tbsp dark soy sauce
2 tsp peanut oil

SAUCE:
2 tbsp vegetable oil
3 garlic cloves, crushed
1 small onion, cut into 8 sections
8 ounces thin green beans, halved
1/4 cup unsalted cashews
1 ounce canned bamboo shoots,
   drained and rinsed

2 tsp dark soy sauce
2 tsp Chinese rice wine or dry
   sherry
1/2 cup beef stock
2 tsp cornstarch
4 tsp water
salt and pepper

1 To make the marinade, mix together the cornstarch, soy sauce and peanut oil.

2 Place the steak in a shallow glass bowl. Pour the marinade over the steak, turn to coat thoroughly, cover, and marinate in the refrigerator for at least 30 minutes.

3 To make the sauce, heat the oil in a preheated wok. Lower the heat slightly, add the garlic, onion, beans, cashews, and bamboo shoots, and stir-fry for 2–3 minutes.

4 Remove the steak from the marinade, drain, add to the wok, and stir-fry for 3–4 minutes.

5 Mix the soy sauce, Chinese rice wine or sherry, and beef stock together. Blend the cornstarch with the water to make a smooth paste and add to the soy sauce mixture, mixing to combine.

6 Stir the mixture into the wok and bring the sauce to a boil, stirring until thickened and clear. Reduce the heat and simmer for 2–3 minutes. Season to taste and serve immediately.

Lamb with Mushroom Sauce

Serves 4

INGREDIENTS

12 ounces lean boneless lamb, such
   as fillet or loin
2 tbsp vegetable oil
3 garlic cloves, crushed
1 leek, sliced

1 tsp cornstarch
4 tbsp light soy sauce
3 tbsp Chinese rice wine or
   dry sherry
3 tbsp water

$\frac{1}{2}$ tsp chili sauce
6 ounces large mushrooms, sliced
$\frac{1}{2}$ tsp sesame oil
fresh red chili strips, to garnish

1 Using a sharp knife, cut
the lamb into thin strips.

2 Heat the oil in a
preheated wok. Add the
lamb strips, garlic, and leek
and stir-fry for about 2–3
minutes.

3 Mix together the
cornstarch, soy sauce,
Chinese rice wine or dry
sherry, water, and chili sauce
in a bowl until thoroughly
combined and set aside.

4 Add the mushrooms to
the wok and stir-fry for
1 minute.

5 Stir in the sauce and
cook for 2–3 minutes,
or until the lamb is cooked
through and tender. Sprinkle
the sesame oil over the top
and transfer to a warm
serving dish. Garnish with
red chili strips and serve
immediately.

COOK'S TIP

*Use rehydrated dried
Chinese mushrooms
obtainable from specialty
shops or Chinese
grocery stores for a really
authentic flavor.*

VARIATION

*The lamb can be replaced
with lean steak or pork
tenderloin in this classic
recipe from Beijing. You
could also use 2–3
scallions, 1 shallot, or 1
small onion instead of
the leek, if desired.*

Sesame Lamb Stir-Fry

Serves 4

INGREDIENTS

1 pound boneless lean lamb

2 tbsp peanut oil

1 carrot, peeled and cut into
matchsticks

2 leeks, sliced

2 garlic cloves, crushed

1/3 cup lamb or vegetable stock

2 tsp light brown sugar

1 tbsp dark soy sauce

4 1/2 tsp sesame seeds

1 Cut the lamb into thin strips. Heat the peanut oil in a preheated wok. Add the lamb and stir-fry for 2–3 minutes. Remove the lamb from the wok with a slotted spoon and set aside.

2 Add the carrot, leek, and garlic to the wok and stir-fry in the remaining oil for 1–2 minutes. Remove from the wok with a slotted spoon and set aside. Drain any remaining oil from the wok.

3 Place the stock, sugar, and soy sauce in the wok and add the lamb.

Cook, stirring constantly to coat the lamb, for 2–3 minutes. Sprinkle the sesame seeds over the top, turning the lamb to coat.

4 Spoon the leek mixture onto a warm serving dish and top with the lamb. Serve immediately.

COOK'S TIP

Be careful not to burn the sugar in the wok when heating and coating the meat, otherwise the flavor of the dish will be spoiled.

VARIATION

This recipe would be equally delicious made with strips of skinless chicken or turkey breast or with shrimp. The cooking times remain the same.

Broiled Ground Lamb

Serves 4

INGREDIENTS

5 tbsp oil
2 onions, sliced
1 pound ground lamb
2 tbsp unsweetened yogurt
1 tsp chili powder
1 tsp finely chopped fresh
    ginger root

1 tsp crushed garlic
1 tsp salt
1½ tsp garam masala
½ tsp ground allspice
2 fresh green chilies
fresh cilantro leaves

TO GARNISH:
1 onion, cut into rings
fresh cilantro leaves, chopped
1 lemon, cut into wedges

1 Heat the oil in a saucepan. Add the onions and sauté until golden brown.

2 Place the ground lamb in a large bowl. Add the yogurt, chili powder, ginger, garlic, salt, garam masala, and ground allspice and mix to combine.

3 Add the lamb mixture to the fried onions and stir-fry for 10–15 minutes. Remove from the heat and set aside.

4 Meanwhile, place the green chilies and half the cilantro leaves in a food processor and process. Alternatively, finely chop the green chilies and cilantro with a sharp knife. Set aside until required.

5 Put the ground lamb mixture in a food processor and process. Alternatively, place in a large bowl and mash with a fork. Mix the lamb mixture with the chilies and cilantro and blend well.

6 Transfer the mixture to a shallow flameproof dish. Cook under a preheated broiler for 10–15 minutes, moving the mixture about with a fork. Watch it carefully to prevent it from burning.

7 Serve garnished with onion rings, cilantro, and lemon wedges.

Ground Lamb with Peas

Serves 4

INGREDIENTS

1 medium onion	2 tomatoes, chopped	1 tsp chili powder
6 tbsp oil	1 tsp salt	1 pound lean ground lamb
3 fresh red chilies	1 tsp finely chopped fresh	1 cup peas
fresh cilantro leaves	ginger root	
	1 tsp crushed garlic	

1 Peel and slice the onion, using a sharp knife.

2 Heat the oil in a medium-size saucepan. Add the onion slices and sauté until golden brown.

3 Add 2 of the red chilies, half of the fresh cilantro leaves, and the chopped tomatoes to the pan and reduce the heat to a simmer.

4 Add the salt, ginger, garlic, and chili powder to the mixture in the pan and stir well to combine.

5 Add the ground lamb to the pan and stir-fry the mixture for 7–10 minutes.

6 Add the peas to the mixture in the pan and cook for a further 3–4 minutes, stirring occasionally.

7 Transfer the lamb and pea mixture to warm serving plates and garnish with the remaining red chili and the fresh cilantro leaves.

COOK'S TIP

The flavor of garlic can be changed according to how it is prepared. For instance, a whole garlic clove added to a dish will give it the flavor but not the "bite" of garlic; a halved clove will add a little bite, a finely chopped garlic clove will release most of the flavor, and a crushed clove will release all of the flavor.

Lean Lamb Cooked in Spinach

Serves 2-4

INGREDIENTS

1³/₄ cups oil
2 medium onions, sliced
¹/₄ bunch fresh cilantro
3 fresh green chilies, chopped
1¹/₂ tsp finely chopped fresh
    ginger root
1¹/₂ tsp crushed garlic
1 tsp chili powder

¹/₂ tsp turmeric
1 pound lean lamb, with or
    without the bone
1 tsp salt
2¹/₄ pounds fresh spinach, trimmed,
    washed, and chopped or
    15 ounce can spinach
3¹/₄ cups water

TO GARNISH:
fresh ginger root, peeled
    and shredded
fresh cilantro leaves

1 Heat the oil in a saucepan and fry the onions until they turn a pale color.

2 Add the fresh cilantro and 2 of the chopped green chilies to the pan and stir-fry for 3–5 minutes.

3 Reduce the heat and add the ginger, garlic, chili powder, and turmeric to the mixture in the pan, stirring to mix.

4 Add the lamb to the pan and stir-fry for a further 5 minutes. Add the salt and the fresh or canned spinach and cook, stirring occasionally with a wooden spoon, for a further 3–5 minutes.

5 Add the water, stirring, and cook over a low heat, covered, for about 45 minutes. Remove the lid and check the meat. If it is not tender, turn it over,

increase the heat, and cook, uncovered, until the surplus water has been absorbed. Stir-fry the mixture for a further 5–7 minutes.

6 Transfer the lamb and spinach mixture to a serving dish and garnish with shredded ginger, fresh cilantro leaves, and the remaining chopped green chili. Serve hot.

Stuffed Tomatoes

Serves 4-6

INGREDIENTS

6 large, firm tomatoes
4 tbsp sweet butter
1 medium onion, finely chopped
5 tbsp oil

1 tsp finely chopped fresh
   ginger root
1 tsp crushed garlic
1 tsp pepper
1 tsp salt

1/2 tsp garam masala
1 pound ground lamb
1 fresh green chili
fresh cilantro leaves

1 Preheat the oven to 350°F. Rinse the tomatoes, cut off the tops, and scoop out the flesh.

2 Grease a heatproof dish with 2 tbsp butter. Place the tomatoes in the dish.

3 Heat the oil in a pan and sauté the onion until golden.

4 Lower the heat and add the ginger, garlic, pepper, salt, and garam masala. Stir-fry the mixture for 3–5 minutes.

5 Add the ground lamb to the saucepan and fry for 10–15 minutes.

6 Add the green chili and fresh cilantro leaves and continue stir-frying the mixture for about 3–5 minutes.

7 Spoon the lamb mixture into the tomatoes and replace the tops. Cook the tomatoes in the oven for 15–20 minutes.

8 Transfer the tomatoes to serving plates and serve hot.

VARIATION

You could use the same recipe to stuff red or green bell peppers, if desired.

Fried Kidneys

Serves 4

INGREDIENTS

1 pound lamb's kidneys	1 tsp finely chopped fresh ginger	1/2 tsp salt
2 tsp turmeric	root	3 tbsp oil
1 green bell pepper, sliced	1 tsp crushed garlic	1 small onion, finely chopped
2/3 cup water	1 tsp chili powder	cilantro leaves, to garnish

1 Using a sharp knife, remove the very fine skin surrounding each kidney. Cut each kidney into 4–6 pieces.

2 Place the kidney pieces in a bowl of warm water with 2 teaspoons of turmeric and 2 teaspoons of salt for about 1 hour. Drain the kidneys thoroughly, then rinse them under cold running water until the water runs clear.

3 Place the kidneys in a small saucepan, together with the green bell pepper. Pour in enough water to cover and cook over a medium heat, leaving the lid of the pan slightly ajar so that the steam can escape, until all the water has evaporated.

4 Add the ginger, garlic, chili powder, and salt to the kidney mixture and blend until well combined.

5 Add the oil, onion, and cilantro to the pan, and stir-fry for 7–10 minutes.

6 Transfer the kidneys to a serving plate and serve hot.

COOK'S TIP

Many people are resistant to the idea of cooking or eating kidneys because they often have a rather strong smell— even when cooked. However, if you wash and soak them in water, you can largely avoid this problem.

Stir-Fried Ginger Chicken

Serves 4

INGREDIENTS

2 tbsp sunflower oil

1 onion, sliced

6 ounces carrots, cut into thin sticks

1 clove garlic, crushed

12 ounces boneless skinless chicken breasts

2 tbsp ginger root, peeled and grated

1 tsp ground ginger

4 tbsp sweet sherry

1 tbsp tomato paste

1 tbsp sugar

½ cup orange juice

1 tsp cornstarch

1 orange, peeled and segmented

fresh snipped chives, to garnish

1 Heat the oil in a large preheated wok. Add the onion, carrots, and garlic and stir-fry over a high heat for 3 minutes, or until the vegetables begin to soften.

2 Using a sharp knife, slice the chicken into thin strips. Add the chicken to the wok, together with the ginger root and ground ginger. Stir-fry for a further 10 minutes, or until the chicken is well cooked through and golden in color.

3 Mix together the sherry, tomato paste,

sugar, orange juice, and cornstarch to a smooth paste in a bowl. Stir the mixture into the wok and heat through until the mixture bubbles and the juices start to thicken.

4 Add the orange segments and carefully toss to mix.

5 Transfer the stir-fried chicken to warm serving bowls and garnish with freshly snipped chives. Serve immediately.

COOK'S TIP

Make sure that you do not continue cooking the dish once the orange segments have been added in step 4, otherwise they will break up.

Chicken, Collard Green, & Yellow Bean Stir-Fry

Serves 4

INGREDIENTS

2 tbsp sunflower oil

1 pound skinless, boneless
   chicken breasts

2 cloves garlic, crushed

1 green bell pepper

1½ cups snow peas

6 scallions, sliced, plus extra
   to garnish

8 ounces collard greens or
   cabbage, shredded

5¾ ounce jar yellow bean sauce

3 tbsp roasted cashew nuts

1 Heat the sunflower oil in a large preheated wok.

2 Using a sharp knife, slice the chicken into thin strips.

3 Add the chicken to the wok, together with the garlic. Stir-fry for about 5 minutes, or until the chicken is sealed on all sides and beginning to turn golden.

4 Using a sharp knife, seed the green bell pepper and cut the flesh into thin strips.

5 Add the snow peas, scallions, green bell pepper strips, and collard greens or cabbage to the wok. Stir-fry for a further 5 minutes, or until the vegetables are just tender.

6 Stir in the yellow bean sauce and heat through for about 2 minutes, or until the mixture starts to bubble.

7 Generously scatter the stir-fry with the roasted cashew nuts.

8 Transfer the chicken, collard green, and yellow bean stir-fry to warm serving plates and garnish with extra scallions, if desired. Serve the stir-fry immediately.

COOK'S TIP

Do not add salted cashew nuts to this dish, otherwise, combined with the slightly salty sauce, the dish will be very salty indeed.

Chicken, Bell Pepper, & Orange Stir-Fry

Serves 4

INGREDIENTS

3 tbsp sunflower oil	1¼ cups snow peas	1 tsp cornstarch
12 ounces skinless, boneless chicken thighs, cut into thin strips	4 tbsp light soy sauce	2 oranges
1 onion, sliced	4 tbsp sherry	½ cup bean sprouts
1 clove garlic, crushed	1 tbsp tomato paste	cooked rice or noodles, to serve
1 red bell pepper, seeded and sliced	finely grated rind and juice of 1 orange	

1 Heat the sunflower oil in a large preheated wok.

2 Add the strips of chicken to the wok and stir-fry for 2–3 minutes, or until sealed on all sides.

3 Add the sliced onion, garlic, bell pepper and snow peas to the wok. Stir-fry the mixture for a further 5 minutes, or until the vegetables are just becoming tender and the chicken is completely cooked through and golden brown.

4 Mix together the soy sauce, sherry, tomato paste, orange rind and juice, and the cornstarch to a smooth paste.

5 Add the mixture to the wok and cook, stirring, until the juices start to thicken.

6 Using a sharp knife, peel and segment the oranges.

7 Add the orange segments and bean sprouts to the mixture in the wok and heat through for a further 2 minutes.

8 Transfer the stir-fry to serving plates and serve at once with cooked rice or noodles.

COOK'S TIP

Bean sprouts are sprouting mung beans and are a regular ingredient in Chinese cooking. They require very little cooking and may even be eaten raw, if desired.

Duck with Baby Corn Cobs & Pineapple

Serves 4

INGREDIENTS

4 duck breasts
1 tsp Chinese five-spice powder
1 tbsp cornstarch
1 tbsp chili oil

8 ounces baby onions, peeled
2 cloves garlic, crushed
1 cup baby corn cobs
1¼ cups canned pineapple chunks

6 scallions, sliced
½ cup bean sprouts
2 tbsp plum sauce

1 Remove any skin from the duck breasts. Cut the duck breasts into thin slices.

2 Mix together the Chinese five-spice powder and the cornstarch in a large bowl.

3 Toss the duck in the five-spice powder and cornstarch mixture until well coated.

4 Heat the oil in a large preheated wok. Stir-fry the duck for about 10 minutes, or until just beginning to go crisp around the edges.

5 Remove the duck from the wok and set aside until it is required.

6 Add the onions and garlic to the wok and stir-fry for 5 minutes, or until the onions have softened.

7 Add the baby corn cobs to the wok and stir-fry for a further 5 minutes.

8 Add the pineapple chunks, scallions, and bean sprouts and stir-fry for 3–4 minutes. Stir in the plum sauce.

9 Return the cooked duck to the wok and toss until well mixed. Transfer to warm serving dishes and serve hot.

COOK'S TIP

Buy pineapple chunks in natural juice rather than syrup for a fresher flavor. If you can obtain only pineapple in syrup, rinse it in cold water and drain thoroughly before using.

Stir-Fried Turkey with Cranberry Glaze

Serves 2–3

INGREDIENTS

1 turkey breast
2 tbsp sunflower oil
2 tbsp preserved ginger

¹/₂ cup fresh or frozen cranberries
¹/₄ cup canned chestnuts
4 tbsp cranberry sauce

3 tbsp light soy sauce
salt and pepper

1 Remove any skin from the turkey breast. Using a sharp knife, thinly slice the turkey breast.

2 Heat the oil in a large preheated wok.

3 Add the turkey to the wok and stir-fry for 5 minutes, or until cooked through.

4 Using a sharp knife, finely chop the preserved ginger.

5 Add the ginger and the cranberries to the wok and stir-fry for 2–3 minutes, or until the cranberries have softened.

6 Add the chestnuts, cranberry sauce, and soy sauce, season to taste with salt and pepper, and allow to bubble for 2–3 minutes.

7 Transfer to warm serving dishes and serve immediately.

COOK'S TIP

If you wish, use a turkey escalope instead of the breast for really tender, lean meat.

COOK'S TIP

It is very important that the wok is very hot before you stir-fry. This can be tested by holding your hand flat about 3 inches above the base of the interior — you should be able to feel the heat radiating from it.

Stir-Fried Beef & Vegetables with Sherry & Soy Sauce

Serves 4

INGREDIENTS

2 tbsp sunflower oil

12 ounces fillet of beef, sliced

1 red onion, sliced

8 ounces zucchini

5 medium carrots, thinly sliced

1 red bell pepper, seeded and sliced

1 small head Chinese cabbage, shredded

¾ cup bean sprouts

8 ounce can bamboo shoots, drained

¾ cup cashew nuts, toasted

SAUCE:

3 tbsp medium sherry

3 tbsp light soy sauce

1 tsp ground ginger

1 clove garlic, crushed

1 tsp cornstarch

1 tbsp tomato paste

1 Heat the sunflower oil in a large preheated wok.

2 Add the beef and onion to the wok and stir-fry for 4–5 minutes, or until the onion begins to soften and the meat is just browning.

3 Using a sharp knife, trim the zucchini and thinly slice diagonally.

4 Add the carrots, bell pepper, and zucchini, and stir-fry for 5 minutes.

5 Toss in the Chinese cabbage, bean sprouts, and bamboo shoots and heat through for 2–3 minutes, or until the cabbage is just beginning to wilt.

6 Scatter the cashews nuts over the stir-fry.

7 To make the sauce, mix together the sherry, soy sauce, ground ginger, garlic, cornstarch, and tomato paste. to make a smooth paste. Pour the sauce over

the stir-fry and toss until well combined. Allow the sauce to bubble for 2–3 minutes, or until the juices start to thicken.

8 Transfer to warm serving dishes and serve at once.

Beef with Green Peas & Black Bean Sauce

Serves 4

INGREDIENTS

1 pound steak

2 tbsp sunflower oil

1 onion

2 cloves garlic, crushed

1¼ cup fresh or frozen peas

5¾ ounce jar black bean sauce

5½ ounces Chinese
  cabbage, shredded

1 Using a sharp knife, trim away any fat from the steak. Cut the steak into thin slices.

2 Heat the sunflower oil in a large preheated wok.

3 Add the steak to the wok and stir-fry for 2 minutes.

4 Using a sharp knife, peel and slice the onion.

5 Add the onion, garlic and peas to the wok and stir-fry for a further 5 minutes.

6 Add the black bean sauce and Chinese cabbage to the mixture in the wok and heat through for a further 2 minutes, or until the cabbage has wilted.

7 Transfer to warm serving bowls and serve immediately.

COOK'S TIP

Chinese cabbage is now widely available. It looks like a pale, elongated head of lettuce with light green, tightly packed crinkly leaves.

COOK'S TIP

Buy a chunky black bean sauce if you can for the best texture and flavor.

Pork Tenderloin Stir-Fry with Crunchy Satay Sauce

Serves 4

INGREDIENTS

2–3 medium carrots

2 tbsp sunflower oil

350g/12 ounces pork tenderloin,
    thinly sliced

1 onion, sliced

2 cloves garlic, crushed

1 yellow bell pepper, seeded
    and sliced

2¹⁄₃ cups snow peas

1¹⁄₂ cups fine asparagus

chopped salted peanuts, to serve

SATAY SAUCE:

6 tbsp crunchy peanut butter

6 tbsp coconut milk

1 tsp chili flakes

1 clove garlic, crushed

1 tsp tomato paste

1 Using a sharp knife, slice the carrots into thin sticks.

2 Heat the oil in a large, preheated wok. Add the pork, onion, and garlic and stir-fry for 5 minutes, or until the lamb is cooked through.

3 Add the carrots, bell pepper, snow peas, and asparagus to the wok and stir-fry for 5 minutes.

4 To make the satay sauce, place the peanut butter, coconut milk, chili flakes, garlic, and tomato paste in a small pan and heat gently, stirring, until well combined.

5 Transfer the stir-fry to warm serving plates. Spoon the satay sauce over the stir-fry and scatter with coarsely chopped peanuts. Serve immediately.

COOK'S TIP

Cook the sauce just before serving as it tends to thicken very quickly and will not be spoonable if you cook it too far in advance.

Spicy Pork Balls

Serves 4

INGREDIENTS

1 pound ground pork	1/2 cup whole-wheat bread crumbs	2 tbsp soy sauce
2 shallots, finely chopped	1 egg, beaten	7 ounce can water chestnuts, drained
2 cloves garlic, crushed	2 tbsp sunflower oil	3 tbsp chopped fresh cilantro
1 tsp cumin seeds	14 ounce can chopped tomatoes,	
1/2 tsp chili powder	flavored with chili	

1 Place the ground pork in a large mixing bowl. Add the shallots, garlic, cumin seeds, chili powder, bread crumbs, and beaten egg and mix together well.

2 Take small pieces of the mixture and form into balls between the palms of your hands.

3 Heat the sunflower oil in a large preheated wok. Add the pork balls to the wok and stir-fry, in batches, over a high heat for about 5 minutes, or until sealed on all sides.

4 Add the tomatoes, soy sauce, and water chestnuts and bring to a boil. Return the pork balls to the wok, reduce the heat and simmer for 15 minutes.

5 Scatter with chopped fresh cilantro, transfer to a serving dish and serve hot.

COOK'S TIP

Add a few teaspoons of chili sauce to a tin of chopped tomatoes, if you can't find the flavored variety.

COOK'S TIP

Cilantro is also known as Chinese parsley, but has a much stronger flavor and should be used with care. Parsley is not a viable alternative; use basil if cilantro is not available.

Twice-Cooked Pork with Bell Peppers

Serves 4

INGREDIENTS

½ ounce Chinese dried mushrooms	1 red bell pepper, seeded	1 yellow bell pepper, seeded
1 pound pork leg steaks	and diced	and diced
2 tbsp vegetable oil	1 green bell pepper, seeded	4 tbsp oyster sauce
1 onion, sliced	and diced	

1 Place the mushrooms in a large bowl. Pour over enough boiling water to cover and let stand for 20 minutes.

2 Using a sharp knife, trim any excess fat from the pork steaks. Cut the pork into thin strips.

3 Bring a large saucepan of water to a boil. Add the pork to the boiling water and cook for 5 minutes.

4 Remove the pork from the pan with a slotted spoon and drain thoroughly.

5 Heat the oil in a large preheated wok. Add the pork to the wok and stir-fry for about 5 minutes.

6 Remove the mushrooms from the water and drain thoroughly. Discard the stalks and chop the mushroom caps.

7 Add the mushrooms, onion, and the bell peppers to the wok and stir-fry for 5 minutes.

8 Stir in the oyster sauce and cook for 2–3 minutes. Transfer to serving bowls and serve immediately.

VARIATION

Use open-cap mushrooms, sliced, instead of Chinese mushrooms, if desired.

Scallion Onion & Lamb Stir-Fry with Oyster Sauce

Serves 4

INGREDIENTS

1 pound lamb leg steaks	2 cloves garlic, crushed	6 tbsp oyster sauce
1 tsp ground Szechuan peppercorns	8 scallions, sliced	6 ounces Chinese cabbage
1 tbsp peanut oil	2 tbsp dark soy sauce	shrimp crackers, to serve

1 Using a sharp knife, remove any excess fat from the lamb. Slice the lamb thinly.

2 Sprinkle the ground Szechuan peppercorns over the meat and toss together until well combined.

3 Heat the oil in a preheated wok. Add the lamb and stir-fry for 5 minutes.

4 Mix the garlic, scallions, and soy sauce, add to the wok, and stir-fry for 2 minutes.

5 Add the oyster sauce and Chinese cabbage and stir-fry for a further 2 minutes, or until the leaves have wilted and the juices are bubbling.

6 Transfer the stir-fry to warm serving bowls and serve hot.

COOK'S TIP

Oyster sauce is made from oysters which are cooked in brine and soy sauce. Sold in bottles, it will keep in the refrigerator for months.

COOK'S TIP

Shrimp crackers consist of compressed slivers of shrimp and flour paste. They expand when deep-fried.

Stir-Fried Lamb with Orange

Serves 4

INGREDIENTS

1 pound ground lamb
2 cloves garlic, crushed
1 tsp cumin seeds
1 tsp ground coriander

1 red onion, sliced
finely grated zest and juice of
1 orange
2 tbsp soy sauce

1 orange, peeled and segmented
salt and pepper
snipped fresh chives, to garnish

1 Add the ground lamb to a preheated wok. Dry fry the ground lamb for 5 minutes, or until the meat is evenly browned. Drain away any excess fat from the wok.

2 Add the garlic, cumin seeds, coriander, and red onion to the wok and stir-fry for a further 5 minutes.

3 Stir in the finely grated orange zest and juice and the soy sauce, cover, reduce the heat, and simmer, stirring occasionally, for 15 minutes.

4 Remove the lid, raise the heat, add the orange segments, and salt and pepper to taste and heat through for a further 2–3 minutes.

5 Transfer to warm serving plates and garnish with snipped fresh chives. Serve immediately.

VARIATION

Use lime or lemon juice and zest instead of the orange, if wished.

COOK'S TIP

If you wish to serve wine with your meal, try light, dry white wines and lighter Burgundy-style red wines as they blend well with Asian food.

Shish Kabobs

Makes 4

INGREDIENTS

1 pound lean lamb
1 red onion, cut into wedges
1 green bell pepper, seeded

MARINADE:
1 onion

4 tbsp olive oil
grated rind and juice of
    1/2 lemon
1 clove garlic, crushed
1/2 tsp dried oregano
1/2 tsp dried thyme

TO SERVE:
4 pita breads
few crisp lettuce leaves,
    shredded
2 tomatoes, sliced
chili sauce (optional)

1 Cut the lamb into large, even-size chunks.

2 To make the marinade, grate the onion or chop it very finely in a food processor. Remove the juice by squeezing the onion between two plates set over a small bowl to collect the juice.

3 Combine the onion juice with the remaining marinade ingredients in a nonmetallic dish and add

the meat. Toss the meat in the marinade, cover, and marinate in the refrigerator for at least 2 hours.

4 Divide the onion wedges into 2. Cut the bell peppers into chunks.

5 Remove the meat from the marinade, reserving the liquid for basting. Thread the meat onto skewers, alternating with the onion and bell peppers. Broil over hot coals for 8–10 minutes, turning and basting frequently.

6 Split the bread; fill with lettuce. Push the meat and vegetables off the skewers into the bread. Top with tomatoes.

VARIATION

These kabobs are delicious served with saffron-flavored rice. For easy saffron rice, simply use saffron stock cubes when cooking the rice.

Lamb Cutlets with Rosemary

Serves 4

INGREDIENTS

8 lamb cutlets
5 tbsp olive oil
2 tbsp lemon juice
1 clove garlic, crushed
1/2 tsp lemon pepper
salt
8 sprigs rosemary

baked potatoes, to serve

SALAD:
4 tomatoes, sliced
4 scallions, sliced diagonally

DRESSING:
2 tbsp olive oil
1 tbsp lemon juice
1 clove garlic, chopped
1/4 tsp fresh rosemary, finely
    chopped

1 Trim the lamb cutlets by cutting away the flesh with a sharp knife to expose the tips of the bones.

2 Place the olive oil, lemon juice, garlic, lemon pepper, and salt in a shallow, nonmetallic dish and whisk with a fork to combine.

3 Lay the sprigs of rosemary in the dish and place the lamb on top. Marinate for at least

1 hour in the refrigerator, turning the cutlets once.

4 Remove the cutlets from the marinade and wrap a little foil around the bones to stop them from burning.

5 Place the sprigs of rosemary on the rack and place the lamb on top. Broil for about 10–15 minutes, turning once.

6 Meanwhile, make the salad and dressing.

Arrange the tomatoes on a serving dish and scatter the scallions on top. Place all the ingredients for the dressing in a screw-top jar, shake well, and pour over the salad. Serve with the broiled lamb cutlets and baked potatoes.

Sweet Lamb Fillet

Serves 4

INGREDIENTS

2 fillets of lamb, 8 ounces
    each
1 tbsp olive oil
1/2 onion, finely chopped
1 clove garlic, crushed
1-inch piece fresh ginger root,
    grated

5 tbsp apple juice
3 tbsp smooth apple sauce
1 tbsp light brown sugar
1 tbsp ketchup
1/2 tsp mild mustard
salt and pepper

salad greens, croutons, and
    fresh crusty bread, to serve

1 Place the lamb fillets on a large piece of double thickness foil. Season with salt and pepper to taste.

2 Heat the oil in a small pan and sauté the onion and garlic for 2–3 minutes, until softened, but not browned. Stir in the grated ginger and cook for 1 minute, stirring occasionally.

3 Stir in the apple juice, apple sauce, sugar, ketchup, and mustard and bring to a boil. Boil rapidly for about 10 minutes, until reduced by half. Stir the mixture occasionally so that it does not burn and stick to the pan.

4 Brush half of the sauce over the lamb, then wrap up the lamb in the foil to completely enclose it. Cook the lamb over hot coals for about 25 minutes, turning the packet over from time to time so that it cooks thoroughly.

5 Open the foil packets and brush the lamb with some of the sauce. Continue to barbecue for another 15–20 minutes, or until cooked through and tender.

6 Place the lamb on a chopping board, remove the foil, and cut into thick slices. Transfer to serving plates and spoon the remaining sauce on top. Serve with salad greens, croutons, and fresh crusty bread.

Caribbean Pork

Serves 4

INGREDIENTS
---

4 pork loin chops
4 tbsp dark brown sugar
4 tbsp orange or pineapple
   juice
2 tbsp Jamaican rum
1 tbsp shredded coconut
1/2 tsp ground cinnamon
mixed salad greens, to serve

COCONUT RICE:
1 generous cup Basmati rice
2 cups water
2/3 cup coconut milk
4 tbsp raisins
4 tbsp roasted peanuts or
   cashew nuts
salt and pepper

2 tbsp shredded coconut,
   toasted

1 Trim any excess fat from the pork and place the chops in a shallow, nonmetallic dish.

2 Combine the sugar, fruit juice, rum, coconut, and cinnamon in a bowl, stirring until the sugar dissolves. Pour the mixture over the pork and marinate in the refrigerator for at least 2 hours.

3 Remove the pork from the marinade,

reserving the liquid for basting. Broil over hot coals for 15–20 minutes, basting with the marinade.

4 Meanwhile, make the coconut rice. Rinse the rice under cold water, place it in a pan with the water and coconut milk, and bring gently to a boil. Stir, cover, and reduce the heat. Simmer for 12 minutes, or until the rice is tender and the liquid has been absorbed. Fluff up with a fork.

5 Stir the raisins and nuts into the rice, season with salt and pepper to taste, and sprinkle with the coconut. Transfer the pork and rice to warm serving plates and serve with the mixed salad greens.

Ham Steaks with Spicy Apple Rings

Serves 4

INGREDIENTS

4 ham steaks, about 6 ounces each
1–2 tsp wholegrain mustard
1 tbsp honey
2 tbsp lemon juice

1 tbsp sunflower oil

APPLE RINGS:
2 green eating apples
2 tsp raw sugar

$^1/_4$ tsp ground nutmeg
$^1/_4$ tsp ground cinnamon
$^1/_4$ tsp ground allspice
1–2 tbsp melted butter

1 Using a pair of scissors, make a few cuts around the edges of the ham steaks to prevent them from curling up as they cook. Spread a little wholegrain mustard over the steaks.

2 Mix the honey, lemon juice, and sunflower oil in a bowl until well combined.

3 To prepare the apple rings, core the apples and cut them into thick slices. Mix the sugar with the spices and press the apple slices in the mixture until well coated on both sides.

4 Broil the steaks over hot coals for 3–4 minutes on each side, basting with the honey and lemon mixture to prevent the meat from drying out during cooking.

5 Brush the apple slices with a little melted butter and broil alongside the meat for about 3–4 minutes, turning once and brushing with melted butter as they cook.

6 Serve with the apple slices as a garnish.

COOK'S TIP

If you have time, soak the steaks in cold water for 30–60 minutes before cooking—this process will remove the excess salt.

Honey-Glazed Pork Chops

Serves 4

INGREDIENTS

4 lean pork loin chops	4 tbsp orange juice	salt and pepper
4 tbsp clear honey	2 tbsp olive oil	
1 tbsp dry sherry	1-inch piece fresh ginger root, grated	

1 Season the pork chops with salt and pepper to taste. Set aside while you make the glaze.

2 To make the glaze, place the honey, sherry, orange juice, oil, and ginger in a small pan and heat gently, stirring continuously, until the ingredients are blended.

3 Broil the chops on an oiled rack over hot coals for about 5 minutes on each side.

4 Brush the chops with the glaze and broil for another 2–4 minutes on each side, basting frequently with the glaze.

5 Transfer the chops to warm serving plates and serve hot.

COOK'S TIP

To give the recipe a little more punch, stir $^1/_2$ teaspoon of chili sauce or 1 tablespoon of wholegrain mustard into the basting glaze.

VARIATION

This recipe works equally well with lamb chops and with chicken portions, such as thighs or drumsticks. Broil the meat in exactly the same way as in this recipe, basting frequently with the honey glaze—the result will be just as delicious!

Liver & Onion Kabobs

Makes 4

INGREDIENTS

12 ounces lamb's liver
2 tbsp seasoned all-purpose
   flour
$^{1}/_{2}$ tsp dried mixed herbs
4$^{1}/_{2}$ ounces bacon

2 medium onions
6 tbsp butter
2 tsp balsamic vinegar

TO SERVE:
mixed salad greens
tomato quarters

1 Using a sharp knife, cut the liver into bite-size pieces. Mix the flour with the dried herbs and toss the liver in the seasoned flour.

2 Stretch out the bacon slices with the back of a knife. Cut each slice in half and wrap the bacon around half of the liver pieces.

3 Thread the plain liver pieces onto skewers, alternating with the bacon-wrapped liver pieces.

4 Cut the onions into rings and thread over the kabobs. Finely chop the onion rings that are too small to thread over the kabobs.

5 Heat the butter in a small pan and sauté the chopped onions for about 5 minutes, until softened. Stir in the vinegar.

6 Brush the butter mixture over the kabobs and broil over hot coals for 8–10 minutes, basting occasionally with the butter mixture, until

the liver is just cooked, but is still a little pink inside.

7 Transfer the kabobs to serving plates. Serve with mixed salad greens and tomatoes.

COOK'S TIP

Choose thick slices of liver to give good-sized pieces. Use bacon to hold 2–3 pieces of thinner liver together if necessary.

Fish & Seafood

The wealth of species and flavors that the world's oceans and rivers provide is immense. Each country combines its local catch with the region's favorite herbs and spices to create a variety of dishes. All of the recipes featured here are easy to prepare and delicious to eat. Moreover, not only are fish and seafood quick to cook but they are packed full with nutritional goodness. Naturally low in fat, yet rich in minerals and proteins, fish and seafood are important to help balance any diet.

The superb recipes in this chapter demonstrate the richness of cooking with fish and seafood. Dishes include modern variations of traditional recipes, such as Macaroni and Prawn Bake and Potato-Topped Cod, and exotic flavors, such as Shrimp Fu Yung and Teriyaki Stir-Fried Salmon with Crispy Leeks. The variety of different fish and the prices of fish and seafood allow you to choose a dish to suit your mood and your wallet.

Sweet & Sour Fish Salad

Serves 4

INGREDIENTS

8 ounces trout fillets
8 ounces white fish fillets
(such as haddock or cod)
1¼ cups water
1 stalk lemon grass
2 lime leaves
1 large red chili
1 bunch scallions, trimmed
and shredded

4 ounces fresh pineapple
flesh, diced
1 small red bell pepper, seeded
and diced
1 bunch watercress, washed
and trimmed
fresh snipped chives, to
garnish

DRESSING:
1 tbsp sunflower oil
1 tbsp rice wine vinegar
pinch of chili powder
1 tsp clear honey
salt and pepper

1 Rinse the fish, place in a skillet, and add the water. Bend the lemon grass in half to bruise it and add to the pan with the lime leaves. Prick the chili with a fork and add to the pan. Bring to a boil and simmer for 7–8 minutes. Let cool.

2 Drain the fish fillet, discarding the lemon grass, lime leaves and chili. Flake the fish flesh away

from the skin, and place in a bowl. Gently stir in the scallions, pineapple, and bell pepper.

3 Arrange the washed watercress on 4 serving plates, spoon the cooked fish mixture on top, and set aside until required.

4 To make the dressing, mix all the ingredients together and season with salt and pepper to taste.

Spoon the dressing over the fish and serve garnished with chives.

VARIATION

This recipe also works very well if you replace the fish with 12 ounces white crabmeat. Add a dash of Tabasco sauce if you like it hot!

Pasta Vongole

Serves 4

INGREDIENTS

1¹/₂ pounds fresh clams or 10 ounce can clams, drained	2 tbsp olive oil	salt and pepper
14 ounces mixed seafood, such as shrimps, squid, and mussels, thawed if frozen	2 cloves garlic, finely chopped	1¹/₂ pounds fresh pasta or 12 ounces dried pasta
	²/₃ cup white wine	
	²/₃ cup fish stock	
	2 tbsp chopped tarragon	

1 If you are using fresh clams, scrub them clean and discard any that are already open.

2 Heat the oil in a large skillet. Add the garlic and the clams to the pan and cook for 2 minutes, shaking the pan to ensure that all the clams are coated in the oil.

3 Add the remaining seafood mixture to the skillet and cook for a further 2 minutes.

4 Pour the wine and stock over the mixed seafood, and bring to a boil. Cover the skillet, reduce the heat, and simmer for 8–10 minutes, or until the shells open. Discard any clams or mussels that do not open.

5 Meanwhile, cook the pasta in a saucepan of boiling water according to the instructions on the packet, or until it is cooked through, but still has "bite." Drain.

6 Stir the tarragon into the sauce and season to taste.

7 Transfer the pasta to a serving dish, pour the sauce over it, and serve.

VARIATION

Red clam sauce can be made by adding 8 tablespoons of tomato sauce along with the stock in step 4. Follow the same cooking method.

Genoese Seafood Risotto

Serves 4

INGREDIENTS

5 cups hot fish or chicken stock
1²/₃ cups risotto rice, washed
3 tbsp butter

2 garlic cloves, chopped
9 ounces mixed, preferably raw,
    seafood, such as jumbo shrimp,
    squid, mussels, clams, and small
    shrimp

2 tbsp chopped oregano, plus extra
    for garnishing
²/₃ cup grated pecorino or
    Parmesan cheese

1 In a large saucepan, bring the stock to a boil. Add the rice and cook, stirring, for about 12 minutes, until the rice is tender or according to the instructions on the packet. Drain thoroughly, reserving any excess liquid.

2 Heat the butter in a large skillet and add the garlic, stirring.

3 Add the raw mixed seafood to the skillet and cook for 5 minutes. If the seafood is already cooked through, sauté for 2–3 minutes.

4 Stir the oregano into the seafood mixture in the skillet.

5 Add the cooked rice to the skillet and cook, stirring constantly, for 2–3 minutes, or until heated through. Add the reserved stock if the mixture gets too sticky.

6 Add the pecorino or Parmesan cheese and mix well.

7 Transfer the risotto to warm serving dishes and serve immediately.

COOK'S TIP

The Genoese are excellent cooks, and they make particularly delicious fish dishes flavored with the local olive oil.

Celery & Salt Cod Casserole

Serves 4

INGREDIENTS

9 ounces salt cod, soaked overnight	3 celery stalks, chopped	1/2 cup pine nuts
1 tbsp oil	14 ounce can tomatoes, chopped	2 tbsp roughly chopped tarragon
4 shallots, finely chopped	2/3 cup fish stock	2 tbsp capers
2 garlic cloves, chopped		crusty bread or mashed potatoes, to serve

1 Drain the salt cod, rinse it under plenty of running water, and drain again thoroughly. Remove and discard any skin and bones. Pat the fish dry with paper towels and cut it into chunks.

2 Heat the oil in a large skillet. Add the shallots and garlic and cook for 2–3 minutes. Add the celery and cook for a further 2 minutes, then add the tomatoes and stock.

3 Bring the mixture to a boil, reduce the heat, and simmer for 5 minutes.

4 Add the fish and cook for 10 minutes, or until tender.

5 Meanwhile, spread the pine nuts out on a cookie sheet. Place under a preheated broiler and toast for 2–3 minutes, or until golden.

6 Stir the tarragon, capers, and pine nuts into the fish casserole and heat gently to warm through.

7 Transfer to serving plates and serve with fresh crusty bread or mashed potatoes.

COOK'S TIP

Salt cod is a useful ingredient to have on hand, and once soaked, can be used in the same way as any other fish. It does, however, have a stronger flavor than normal, and it is, of course, slightly salty. It can be found in fish markets, larger supermarkets, and delicatessens.

Salt Cod Fritters

Makes 28 cakes

INGREDIENTS

³/₄ cup self-rising flour	1 small red onion, finely chopped	TO SERVE:
1 egg, beaten	1 small fennel bulb, finely chopped	crisp salad, chili relish, cooked rice,
²/₃ cup milk	1 fresh red chili, finely chopped	and fresh vegetables
9 ounces salt cod, soaked overnight	2 tbsp oil	

1 Sift the flour into a large bowl. Make a well in the center of the flour and add the egg.

2 Using a wooden spoon, gradually draw in the flour, slowly adding the milk, and mix to form a smooth batter. Let stand for 10 minutes.

3 Drain the salt cod and rinse it in under running water. Drain again thoroughly.

4 Remove and discard the skin and any bones from the fish, then mash the flesh with a fork.

5 Place the fish in a large bowl and combine with the onion, fennel, and chili. Add the mixture to the batter and blend together.

6 Heat the oil in a large skillet and, taking about 1 tablespoon of the mixture at a time, spoon it into the hot oil. Cook the fritters, in batches, for 3–4 minutes on each side, until golden and slightly puffed. Keep warm while cooking the remaining mixture.

7 Serve with salad and a chili relish for a light meal or with vegetables and rice.

COOK'S TIP

If you prefer larger fritters, use 2 tablespoons per fritter and cook for slightly longer.

Herrings with Hot Pesto Sauce

Serves 4

INGREDIENTS

4 herrings or small mackerel, cleaned and gutted	8 ounces tomatoes, peeled, seeded, and chopped	about 30 fresh basil leaves
2 tbsp olive oil	8 canned anchovy fillets, chopped	½ cup pine nuts
		2 garlic cloves, crushed

1 Cook the herrings under a preheated broiler for about 8-10 minutes on each side, or until the skin is slightly charred on both sides.

2 Meanwhile, heat 1 tablespoon of the olive oil in a large saucepan.

3 Add the tomatoes and anchovies to the saucepan and cook over a medium heat for 5 minutes.

4 Meanwhile, place the basil, pine nuts, garlic, and remaining oil into a food processor and blend to form a smooth paste.

Alternatively, pound the ingredients by hand in a mortar with a pestle.

5 Add the pesto mixture to the saucepan containing the tomato and anchovy mixture, and stir to heat through.

6 Spoon some of the pesto sauce onto warm individual serving plates. Place the fish on top and pour the rest of the pesto sauce over the fish. Serve immediately.

COOK'S TIP

Try barbecuing the fish for an extra charbroiled flavor, if desired.

Sole Fillets in Marsala & Cream

Serves 4

INGREDIENTS

STOCK:

2½ cups water

bones and skin from the sole fillets

1 onion, peeled and halved

1 carrot, peeled and halved

3 fresh bay leaves

SAUCE:

1 tbsp olive oil

1 tbsp butter

4 shallots, finely chopped

3½ ounces baby button
    mushrooms, wiped and halved

1 tbsp peppercorns, lightly crushed

8 sole fillets

⅓ cup Marsala

⅔ pint heavy cream

1 To make the stock, place the water, fish bones and skin, onion, carrot, and bay leaves in a saucepan and bring to a boil.

2 Reduce the heat and simmer the mixture for 1 hour, or until the stock has reduced to about ⅔ cup. Drain the stock through a fine strainer, discarding the bones and vegetables, and set aside.

3 To make the sauce, heat the oil and butter in a skillet. Add the shallots and cook, stirring occasionally, for 2–3 minutes, or until just softened.

4 Add the mushrooms to the skillet and cook, stirring occasionally, for a further 2–3 minutes, or until they are just beginning to brown.

5 Add the peppercorns and sole fillets to the skillet. Fry the sole fillets for 3–4 minutes on each side, or until a golden brown color.

6 Pour the wine and stock over the fish and simmer for 3 minutes.

Remove the fish with a fish slice or a slotted spoon, set aside, and keep warm.

7 Increase the heat and boil the mixture in the skillet for about 5 minutes, or until the sauce has reduced and thickened.

8 Pour in the cream, return the fish to the skillet, and heat through. Serve with cooked vegetables of your choice.

Fresh Baked Sardines

Serves 4

INGREDIENTS

2 tbsp olive oil	8 sardine fillets or about 2¹/₄ pounds	4 eggs, beaten
2 large onions, sliced into rings	sardines, filleted	²/₃ pint milk
3 garlic cloves, chopped	1 cup grated Parmesan cheese	salt and pepper
2 large zucchini, cut into sticks		
3 tbsp fresh thyme, stalks removed		

1 Heat 1 tablespoon of the olive oil in a skillet. Add the onion rings and chopped garlic and sauté for about 2–3 minutes.

2 Add the zucchini to the skillet and cook, stirring occasionally, for about 5 minutes, or until golden.

3 Stir 2 tablespoons of thyme into the mixture.

4 Place half the onions and zucchini in the base of a large ovenproof dish. Top with the sardine fillets and half the grated Parmesan cheese.

5 Place the remaining onions and zucchini on top and sprinkle with the remaining thyme.

6 Mix the eggs and milk together in a bowl and season to taste with salt and pepper. Pour the mixture over the vegetables and sardines in the dish. Sprinkle the remaining Parmesan cheese over the top.

7 Bake in a preheated oven at 350°F for 20–25 minutes, or until golden and set. Serve the fresh baked sardines hot, straight from the oven.

VARIATION

If you cannot find sardines that are large enough to fillet, use small mackerel instead.

Marinated Fish

Serves 4

INGREDIENTS

4 mackerel	2 tbsp extra-virgin olive oil	2 garlic cloves, crushed
4 tbsp chopped marjoram	finely grated rind and juice of 1 lime	salt and pepper

1 Under gently running water, scrape the mackerel with the blunt side of a knife to remove any scales.

2 Using a sharp knife, make a slit in the stomach of the fish and cut horizontally along until the knife will go no farther very easily. Gut the fish and rinse under water. You may prefer to remove the heads before cooking, but it is not necessary.

3 Using a sharp knife, cut 4–5 diagonal slashes on each side of the fish. Place the fish in a shallow, nonmetallic dish.

4 To make the marinade, mix together the marjoram, olive oil, lime rind and juice, garlic, and salt and pepper in a bowl.

5 Pour the mixture over the fish. Marinate in the refrigerator for 30 minutes.

6 Cook the mackerel, under a preheated broiler, for 5–6 minutes on each side, brushing occasionally with the reserved marinade, until golden.

7 Transfer the fish to serving plates. Pour over any remaining marinade before serving.

COOK'S TIP

If the lime is too hard to squeeze, microwave on high for 30 seconds to release the juice. This dish is also excellent cooked on the grill.

Mussel Casserole

Serves 4

INGREDIENTS

2¼ pounds mussels	1 onion, finely chopped	3½ ounces tomato sauce
⅔ cup white wine	3 garlic cloves, chopped	1 tbsp chopped marjoram
1 tbsp oil	1 red chili, finely chopped	toast or crusty bread, to serve

1 Scrub the mussels to remove any mud or sand.

2 Remove the beards from the mussels by pulling away the hairy protrusion between the two shells. Rinse the mussels in a bowl of clean water. Discard any mussels that do not close when they are tapped – they are dead and should not be eaten.

3 Place the mussels in a large saucepan. Pour in the wine and cook for 5 minutes, shaking the pan occasionally until the shells open. Remove and discard any mussels that do not open.

4 Remove the mussels from the saucepan with a slotted spoon. Strain the cooking liquid through a fine strainer set over a bowl, reserving the cooking liquid.

5 Heat the oil in a large skillet. Add the onion, garlic, and chili and cook for 4–5 minutes, or until softened.

6 Add the reserved cooking liquid to the pan and cook for 5 minutes, or until reduced.

7 Stir in the tomato sauce, marjoram, and mussels and cook until hot.

8 Transfer to serving bowls and serve with toast or plenty of crusty bread to mop up the juices.

COOK'S TIP

Finger bowls are individual bowls of warm water with a slice of lemon floating in them. They are used to clean your fingers at the end of a meal.

Sea Bass with Olive Sauce on a Bed of Macaroni

Serves 4

INGREDIENTS

1 pound dried macaroni	SAUCE:	juice of 1 lemon
1 tbsp olive oil	2 tbsp butter	salt and pepper
8 4-ounce sea bass medallions	4 shallots, chopped	
	2 tbsp capers	
	1 1/2 cups pitted green olives,	
TO GARNISH:	chopped	
lemon slices	4 tbsp balsamic vinegar	
shredded leek	1 1/4 cups fish stock	
shredded carrot	1 1/4 cups heavy cream	

1 To make the sauce, melt the butter in a skillet and fry the shallots for 4 minutes. Add the capers and olives and cook for 3 minutes longer.

2 Stir in the balsamic vinegar and fish stock, bring to a boil, and reduce by half. Add the cream, stirring, and reduce again by half. Season to taste and stir in the lemon juice. Remove from the heat, set aside, and keep warm.

3 Bring a pan of salted water to a boil. Add the pasta and olive oil and cook for 12 minutes, until tender but still firm to the bite.

4 Meanwhile, lightly broil the sea bass medallions for 3–4 minutes on each side, until cooked through, but still moist and delicate.

5 Drain the pasta and transfer to a large serving dish. Top the pasta with the fish medallions and then pour on the olive sauce. Garnish with a few lemon slices, shredded leek, and shredded carrot and serve immediately.

Vermicelli with Fillets of Red Mullet

Serves 4

INGREDIENTS

2¼ pounds red mullet fillets
1¼ cups dry white wine
4 shallots, finely chopped
1 garlic clove, crushed
3 tbsp mixed fresh herbs
finely grated rind and juice of
   1 lemon

pinch of freshly grated
   nutmeg
3 anchovy fillets, roughly
   chopped
2 tbsp heavy cream
1 tsp cornstarch
1 pound dried vermicelli

1 tbsp olive oil
salt and pepper

TO GARNISH:
1 fresh mint sprig
lemon slices
lemon rind

1 Put the fish fillets in a large casserole. Pour the wine over and add the shallots, garlic, chopped herbs, lemon rind and juice, nutmeg, and anchovies. Season to taste. Cover and bake in a preheated oven at 350°F for 35 minutes.

2 Carefully transfer the mullet to a warm dish. Set aside and keep warm while you prepare the sauce and pasta.

3 Pour the cooking liquid into a pan and bring to a boil. Simmer for 25 minutes, until reduced by half. Mix together the cream and cornstarch and stir into the sauce to thicken.

4 Bring a pan of salted water to a boil. Add the vermicelli and olive oil and cook until tender, but still firm to the bite. Drain the pasta and transfer to a warm serving dish.

5 Arrange the red mullet fillets on top of the vermicelli and pour the sauce over it. Garnish with a fresh mint sprig, slices of lemon, and strips of lemon rind and serve immediately.

COOK'S TIP

The best red mullet is sometimes called golden mullet, although it is bright red in color.

Spaghetti al Tonno

Serves 4

INGREDIENTS
---

7 ounce can tuna, drained
2 ounce can anchovies, drained
1 1/8 cups olive oil

1 cup roughly chopped parsley
5/8 cup crème fraîche
1 pound dried spaghetti
2 tbsp butter
salt and pepper

black olives, to garnish
crusty bread, to serve

---

1 Remove any bones from the tuna. Put the tuna into a food processor or blender, together with the anchovies, 1 cup of the olive oil, and the parsley. Process until smooth.

2 Spoon the crème fraîche into the food processor or blender and process again for a few seconds to blend. Season to taste.

3 Bring a large pan of lightly salted water to a boil. Add the spaghetti and the remaining olive oil and cook until tender, but still firm to the bite.

4 Drain the spaghetti, return to the saucepan and place over a medium heat. Add the butter and toss well to coat. Spoon in the sauce and quickly toss into the spaghetti, using 2 forks, until well combined.

5 Remove the pan from the heat and divide the spaghetti between 4 warm individual plates. Garnish with the olives and serve immediately with warm, crusty bread.

VARIATION

If desired, you could add 1–2 garlic cloves to the sauce, substitute 1/2 cup chopped fresh basil for half the parsley, and garnish with capers instead of black olives.

Casserole of Fusilli & Smoked Haddock with Egg Sauce

Serves 4

INGREDIENTS

2 tbsp butter, plus extra
   for greasing
1 pound smoked haddock
   fillets, cut into 4 slices
2 1/2 cups milk
1/4 cup all-purpose flour

pinch of freshly grated
   nutmeg
3 tbsp heavy cream
1 tbsp chopped fresh parsley,
   plus extra to garnish

2 eggs, hard cooked and
   mashed to a pulp
4 cups dried fusilli
1 tbsp lemon juice
salt and pepper
boiled new potatoes and
   beets, to serve

1 Grease a casserole with butter. Put the haddock in the casserole and pour in the milk. Bake in a preheated oven at 400°F for 15 minutes. Carefully pour the cooking liquid into a pitcher without breaking up the fish.

2 Melt the butter in a saucepan and stir in the flour. Gradually whisk in the reserved cooking liquid. Season with salt, pepper, and nutmeg. Stir in the cream, parsley, and mashed egg and cook for 2 minutes.

3 Bring a large saucepan of lightly salted water to a boil. Add the fusilli and lemon juice and cook until tender, but still firm to the bite.

4 Drain the pasta and tip it over the fish. Top with the sauce and return to the oven for 10 minutes.

5 Garnish and serve the casserole with boiled new potatoes and beets.

VARIATION

You can use any type of dried pasta for this casserole. Try penne, conchiglie, or rigatoni.

Poached Salmon Steaks with Penne

Serves 4

INGREDIENTS

4 10-ounce fresh salmon
    steaks
4 tbsp butter
$^3/_4$ cup dry white wine
sea salt
8 peppercorns
fresh dill sprig
fresh tarragon sprig
1 lemon, sliced

1 pound dried penne
2 tbsp olive oil
lemon slices and fresh
    watercress, to garnish

LEMON & WATERCRESS
    SAUCE:
2 tbsp butter
$^1/_4$ cup all-purpose flour

$^5/_8$ cup warm milk
juice and finely grated rind of
    2 lemons
2 ounces watercress, chopped
salt and pepper

1 Put the salmon in a large, nonstick pan. Add the butter, wine, a pinch of sea salt, the peppercorns, dill, tarragon, and lemon. Cover, bring to a boil, and simmer for 10 minutes.

2 Using a fish slice, remove the salmon. Strain and reserve the cooking liquid. Remove and discard the salmon skin and center bones.

Place the fish on a warm dish, cover, and keep warm.

3 Bring a saucepan of salted water to a boil. Add the penne and 1 tbsp of the oil and cook for 12 minutes. Drain and toss in the remaining olive oil. Place on a warm serving dish, top with the salmon steaks, and keep warm.

4 To make the sauce, melt the butter and stir

in the flour for 2 minutes. Stir in the milk and about 7 tbsp of the reserved cooking liquid. Add the lemon juice and rind and cook, stirring, for 10 minutes.

5 Add the watercress to the sauce, stir gently, and season to taste.

6 Pour the sauce over the salmon and penne, garnish, and serve.

Spaghetti with Smoked Salmon

Serves 4

INGREDIENTS

1 pound dried buckwheat
    spaghetti
2 tbsp olive oil
¹/₂ cup crumbled feta cheese
salt
fresh cilantro or parsley leaves,
    to garnish

SAUCE:
1¹/₄ cups heavy cream
⁵/₈ cup whiskey or brandy
4¹/₂ ounces smoked salmon
pinch of cayenne pepper
black pepper

2 tbsp chopped fresh cilantro
    or parsley

---

1 Bring a large pan of lightly salted water to a boil. Add the spaghetti and 1 tbsp of the olive oil and cook until tender, but still firm to the bite. Drain and toss in the remaining olive oil. Cover, shake the pan, set aside, and keep warm.

2 Pour the cream into a small saucepan and bring to simmering point, but do not let it boil. Pour the whiskey or brandy into another small saucepan and bring to simmering point, but do not allow it to boil. Remove both pans from the heat and mix together the cream and whiskey or brandy.

3 Cut the smoked salmon into thin strips and add to the cream mixture. Season to taste with cayenne and black pepper. Just before serving, add the chopped fresh cilantro or parsley and stir until well combined.

4 Transfer the spaghetti to a warm serving dish, pour the sauce on, and toss thoroughly with 2 large forks. Scatter the crumbled feta cheese over the top, garnish with the cilantro or parsley leaves, and serve immediately.

COOK'S TIP

Serve this rich and luxurious dish with a green salad tossed in a lemony dressing.

Spaghetti with Seafood Sauce

Serves 4

INGREDIENTS

8 ounces dried spaghetti,
 broken into 6-inch lengths
2 tbsp olive oil
1 1/4 cups chicken stock
1 tsp lemon juice
1 small cauliflower, cut into
 florets
2 carrots, thinly sliced
14 ounces snow peas

4 tbsp butter
1 onion, sliced
8 ounces zucchini, sliced
1 garlic clove, chopped
12 ounces frozen, cooked,
 peeled shrimp, defrosted
2 tbsp chopped fresh parsley
1/3 cup freshly grated
 Parmesan cheese

1/2 tsp paprika
salt and pepper
4 unpeeled, cooked shrimp,
 to garnish

1 Bring a pan of salted water to a boil. Add the spaghetti and 1 tbsp of the olive oil and cook until tender, but still firm to the bite. Drain and toss with the remaining olive oil, cover, and keep warm.

2 Bring the chicken stock and lemon juice to a boil. Add the cauliflower and carrots and cook for 3–4 minutes.

Remove from the pan and set aside. Add the snow peas to the pan and cook for 1–2 minutes. Set aside with the other vegetables.

3 Melt half of the butter in a skillet and sauté the onion and zucchini for about 3 minutes. Add the garlic and shrimp to the skillet and cook for a further 2–3 minutes, until thoroughly heated through.

Stir in the reserved vegetables and heat through. Season with salt and pepper to taste and stir in the remaining butter.

4 Transfer the pasta to a warm serving dish. Pour over the sauce and add the parsley. Toss well and sprinkle with the Parmesan and paprika, garnish with the unpeeled shrimp, and serve.

Macaroni & Shrimp Bake

Serves 4

INGREDIENTS

3 cups dried short-cut
macaroni

1 tbsp olive oil, plus extra
for brushing

6 tbsp butter, plus extra for
greasing

2 small fennel bulbs, thinly
sliced and fronds reserved

6 ounces mushrooms, thinly
sliced

6 ounces peeled, cooked
shrimp

pinch of cayenne pepper

1$\frac{1}{4}$ cups Béchamel sauce (see
Cook's Tip)

$\frac{2}{3}$ cup freshly grated
Parmesan cheese

2 large tomatoes, sliced

1 tsp dried oregano

salt and pepper

1 Bring a saucepan of salted water to a boil. Add the pasta and oil and cook until tender, but still firm to the bite. Drain and return to the pan. Add 2 tbsp of butter, cover, shake the pan, and keep warm.

2 Melt the remaining butter in a pan. Sauté the fennel for 3–4 minutes. Stir in the mushrooms and cook for 2 minutes. Stir in the shrimp, then remove the pan from the heat.

3 Stir the pasta, cayenne pepper and shrimp mixture into the béchamel sauce. Pour into a greased ovenproof dish. Sprinkle with the Parmesan cheese and arrange the tomato slices around the edge. Brush the tomatoes with olive oil and sprinkle the oregano on top.

4 Bake in a preheated oven at 350°F for 25 minutes, until golden brown. Serve immediately.

COOK'S TIP

For béchamel sauce, melt 2 tbsp butter. Stir in $\frac{1}{4}$ cup flour. Cook, stirring, for 2 minutes. Gradually, stir in 1$\frac{1}{4}$ cups warm milk. Add 2 tbsp finely chopped onion, 5 white peppercorns, and 2 parsley sprigs, and season with salt, dried thyme, and grated nutmeg. Simmer, stirring, for 15 minutes. Strain before using.

Pasta Packets

Serves 4

INGREDIENTS
---

1 pound dried fettuccine	1 pound 10 ounces large raw	$^1/_2$ cup dry white wine
$^5/_8$ cup pesto sauce (see page 12)	shrimp, peeled and deveined	salt and pepper
4 tsp extra virgin olive oil	2 garlic cloves, crushed	lemon wedges, to serve

1 Cut out 4 × 12-inch squares of baking paper.

2 Bring a large saucepan of lightly salted water to a boil. Add the fettuccine and cook for 2–3 minutes, until just softened. Drain thoroughly, keep warm, and set aside.

3 Mix together the fettuccine and half of the pesto sauce. Spread out the paper squares and put 1 tsp olive oil in the middle of each. Divide the fettuccine between the squares, then divide the shrimp, and place on top of the fettuccine.

4 Mix together the remaining pesto sauce and the garlic and spoon it over the shrimp. Season each packet with salt and black pepper and sprinkle with the white wine.

5 Dampen the edges of the baking paper and wrap the packets loosely, twisting the edges to seal.

6 Place the packets on a cookie sheet and bake in a preheated oven at 400°F for about 10–15 minutes. Transfer the packets to 4 warm individual plates and serve with lemon wedges.

COOK'S TIP

Traditionally, these packets are designed to look like old-fashioned money bags. The resemblance is more effective with baking paper than with foil.

Pasta Shells with Mussels

Serves 4–6

INGREDIENTS

2³/₄ pounds mussels
1 cup dry white wine
2 large onions, chopped
¹/₂ cup unsalted butter

6 large garlic cloves, finely
chopped
5 tbsp chopped fresh parsley
1¹/₄ cups heavy cream
14 ounces dried pasta shells

1 tbsp olive oil
salt and pepper
crusty bread, to serve

1 Scrub and debeard the mussels under cold running water. Discard any that do not close when sharply tapped. Put the mussels into a large saucepan with the wine and half of the onions. Cover and cook over a medium heat until the shells open.

2 Remove the pan from the heat. Drain the mussels and reserve the cooking liquid. Discard any mussels that have not opened. Strain the cooking liquid and reserve.

3 Melt the butter in a pan and sauté the remaining onion until translucent. Stir in the garlic and cook for 1 minute. Gradually stir in the reserved cooking liquid, then the parsley and cream. Season and simmer.

4 Cook the pasta with the oil until just tender, but still firm to the bite. Drain, return to the pan, cover and keep warm.

5 Reserve a few mussels for the garnish and remove the remainder from their shells. Stir the shelled mussels into the cream sauce and warm briefly. Transfer the pasta to a serving dish. Pour the sauce over the pasta and toss to coat. Garnish with the reserved mussels and serve with bread.

COOK'S TIP

Pasta shells are ideal because the sauce collects in the cavities and impregnates the pasta with flavor.

Saffron Mussel Tagliatelle

Serves 4

INGREDIENTS

2¹/₄ pounds mussels
⁵/₈ cup white wine
1 medium onion, finely
    chopped
2 tbsp butter
2 garlic cloves, crushed
2 tsp cornstarch

1¹/₄ cups heavy cream
pinch of saffron threads or
    saffron powder
1 egg yolk
juice of ¹/₂ lemon
1 pound dried tagliatelle
1 tbsp olive oil

salt and pepper
3 tbsp chopped fresh parsley,
    to garnish

1 Scrub and debeard the mussels under cold running water. Discard any that do not close when sharply tapped. Put the mussels in a pan with the wine and onion. Cover and cook over a high heat until the shells open.

2 Drain and reserve the cooking liquid. Discard any mussels that are still closed. Reserve a few mussels for the garnish and remove the remainder from their shells.

3 Strain the cooking liquid into a saucepan. Bring to a boil and reduce by about half. Remove the pan from the heat.

4 Melt the butter in a saucepan and fry the garlic for 2 minutes, until golden brown. Stir in the cornstarch and cook, stirring, for 1 minute. Gradually stir in the cooking liquid and the cream. Crush the saffron threads and add to the pan. Season to taste and simmer

for 2–3 minutes, until the sauce has thickened.

5 Stir in the egg yolk, lemon juice, and shelled mussels. Do not allow the mixture to boil.

6 Bring a pan of salted water to a boil. Add the pasta and oil and cook until tender. Drain and transfer to a serving dish. Add the mussel sauce and toss. Garnish with the parsley and reserved mussels and serve.

Vermicelli with Clams

Serves 4

INGREDIENTS

14 ounces dried vermicelli, spaghetti, or other long pasta	2 7-ounce jars clams in water	TO GARNISH:
2 tbsp olive oil	$^1/_2$ cup white wine	2 tbsp Parmesan cheese shavings
2 tbsp butter	4 tbsp chopped fresh parsley	fresh basil sprigs
2 onions, chopped	$^1/_2$ tsp dried oregano	
2 garlic cloves, chopped	pinch of freshly grated nutmeg	
	salt and pepper	

1 Bring a large pan of lightly salted water to a boil. Add the pasta and half the olive oil and cook until tender, but still firm to the bite. Drain, return to the pan, and add the butter. Cover the pan, shake well, and keep warm.

2 Heat the remaining oil in a pan over a medium heat. Add the onions and sauté until they are translucent. Stir in the garlic and cook for 1 minute.

3 Strain the liquid from 1 jar of clams and add the liquid to the pan, with the wine. Stir, bring to simmering point, and simmer for 3 minutes. Drain the second jar of clams and discard the liquid.

4 Add the clams, parsley, and oregano to the pan and season with pepper and nutmeg. Lower the heat and cook until the sauce is completely heated through.

5 Transfer the pasta to a serving dish and pour over the sauce. Garnish and serve immediately.

COOK'S TIP

There are many different types of clams found along almost every coast in the world. Those traditionally used in this dish are the very tiny ones—only 1–2 inches across—known in Italy as vongole.

Squid & Macaroni Stew

Serves 4–6

INGREDIENTS

2 cups dried short-cut
    macaroni or other small
    pasta shapes
7 tbsp olive oil
2 onions, sliced
12 ounces prepared squid, cut
    into $1^1/_2$-inch strips

1 cup fish stock
$^5/_8$ cup red wine
12 ounces tomatoes, skinned
    and thinly sliced
2 tbsp tomato paste
1 tsp dried oregano
2 bay leaves

2 tbsp chopped fresh parsley
salt and pepper
crusty bread, to serve

1 Bring a large pan of lightly salted water to a boil. Add the pasta and 1 tbsp of the olive oil and cook for 3 minutes. Drain and keep warm.

2 Heat the remaining oil in a pan and sauté the onions until translucent. Add the squid and stock and simmer for 5 minutes. Pour in the wine, tomatoes, tomato paste, oregano, and bay leaves. Bring the sauce to a boil, season to taste, and cook for 5 minutes.

3 Stir the pasta into the pan, cover, and simmer for about 10 minutes, or until the squid and macaroni are tender and the sauce has thickened. If the sauce remains too liquid, uncover the pan and continue cooking for a few minutes.

4 Discard the bay leaves. Reserve a little parsley and stir the remainder into the pan. Transfer to a warm serving dish and sprinkle with the remaining parsley. Serve with crusty bread.

COOK'S TIP

To prepare squid, peel off the outer skin, then cut off the head and tentacles. Extract the transparent flat oval bone from the body and discard. Remove the sac of black ink, then turn the body sac inside out. Wash in cold water. Cut off the tentacles and discard the rest; wash thoroughly.

Steamed Fish with Black Bean Sauce

Serves 4

INGREDIENTS

2 pounds whole snapper, cleaned
    and scaled
3 garlic cloves, crushed
2 tbsp black bean sauce
1 tsp cornstarch

2 tsp sesame oil
2 tbsp light soy sauce
2 tsp superfine sugar
2 tbsp Chinese rice wine or
    dry sherry
1 small leek, shredded

1 small red bell pepper, seeded and
    cut into thin strips
shredded leek and lemon wedges,
    to garnish
boiled rice or noodles, to serve

1 Rinse the fish inside and out with cold running water and pat dry with paper towels. Make 2-3 diagonal slashes in the flesh on each side of the fish, using a sharp knife. Rub the garlic into the fish.

2 Thoroughly mix the black bean sauce, cornstarch, sesame oil, light soy sauce, sugar, and Chinese rice wine or dry sherry together in a bowl. Place the fish in a shallow heatproof dish and pour the sauce mixture over the top.

3 Sprinkle the leek and bell pepper strips on top of the sauce. Place the dish in the top of a steamer, cover, and steam for 10 minutes, or until the fish is cooked through. Transfer to a serving dish, garnish with shredded leek and lemon wedges, and serve with rice or noodles.

VARIATION

Whole sea bream or sea bass may be used in this recipe instead of snapper, if desired.

COOK'S TIP

Insert the point of a sharp knife into the fish to test if it is cooked. The fish is cooked through if the knife goes into the flesh easily.

Trout with Pineapple

Serves 4

INGREDIENTS

4 trout fillets, skinned	1 celery stalk, sliced	1 tsp cornstarch
2 tbsp vegetable oil	1 tbsp light soy sauce	2 tsp water
2 garlic cloves, cut into slivers	1/4 cup fresh or unsweetened	shredded celery leaves and fresh red
4 slices fresh pineapple, peeled	pineapple juice	chili strips, to garnish
and diced	2/3 cup fish stock	

1 Cut the trout fillets into strips. Heat 1 tablespoon of the vegetable oil in a preheated wok until almost smoking. Reduce the heat slightly, add the fish, and sauté for 2 minutes. Remove from the wok and set aside.

2 Add the remaining oil to the wok, reduce the heat, and add the garlic, pineapple, and celery. Stir-fry for 1–2 minutes.

3 Add the soy sauce, pineapple juice, and fish stock to the wok. Bring to a boil and cook, stirring, for 2–3 minutes, or until the sauce has reduced.

4 Blend the cornstarch with the water to form a smooth paste and stir it into the wok. Bring the sauce to a boil and cook, stirring constantly, until the sauce has thickened and cleared.

5 Return the fish to the wok, and cook, stirring gently, until heated through. Transfer to a warm serving dish and serve, garnished with shredded celery leaves and red chili strips.

COOK'S TIP

Use canned pineapple instead of fresh pineapple if desired, choosing slices in unsweetened, natural juice instead of syrup.

Mullet with Ginger

Serves 4

INGREDIENTS

1 whole mullet, cleaned and scaled
2 scallions, chopped
1 tsp grated fresh ginger root
$^1/_2$ cup garlic wine vinegar
$^1/_2$ cup light soy sauce

3 tsp superfine sugar
dash of chili sauce
$^1/_2$ cup fish stock
1 green bell pepper, seeded and
thinly sliced

1 large tomato, peeled, seeded, and
cut into thin strips
salt and pepper
sliced tomato, to garnish

1 Rinse the fish inside and out and pat thoroughly dry with paper towels.

2 Make 3 diagonal slits in the flesh on each side of the fish. Season with salt and pepper inside and out.

3 Place the fish on a heatproof plate and scatter the chopped scallions and grated ginger over the top. Cover and steam for 10 minutes, or until the fish is cooked through.

4 Meanwhile, place the garlic wine vinegar, soy sauce, sugar, chili sauce, fish stock, bell pepper, and tomato in a saucepan and bring to a boil, stirring occasionally. Cook over a high heat until the sauce has slightly reduced and thickened.

5 Remove the fish from the steamer and transfer to a warm serving dish. Pour the sauce over the fish, garnish with tomato slices, and serve immediately.

COOK'S TIP

Use fillets of fish for this recipe if desired, and reduce the cooking time to 5–7 minutes.

Seafood Medley

Serves 4

INGREDIENTS

2 tbsp dry white wine
1 egg white, lightly beaten
$1/2$ tsp Chinese five-spice powder
1 tsp cornstarch
$10^1/2$ ounces raw shrimp, peeled and deveined

$4^1/2$ ounces prepared squid, cut into rings
$4^1/2$ ounces white fish fillets, cut into strips
vegetable oil, for deep-frying

1 green bell pepper, seeded and cut into thin strips
1 carrot, peeled and cut into thin strips
4 baby corncobs, halved lengthwise

1 Mix together the wine, egg white, Chinese five-spice powder, and cornstarch in a large bowl, combining well. Add the shrimp, squid rings, and fish fillets and stir gently to coat thoroughly and evenly. Remove the fish and seafood with a slotted spoon, reserving any leftover wine and cornstarch mixture.

2 Heat the oil in a preheated wok. Add the shrimp, squid, and fish strips and deep-fry for 2–3 minutes. Remove the seafood mixture from the wok with a slotted spoon and set aside.

3 Pour off all but 1 tablespoon of oil from the wok and return to the heat. Add the bell pepper, carrot, and corncobs and stir-fry for 4–5 minutes.

4 Return the seafood mixture to the wok and add any remaining wine and cornstarch mixture. Cook, stirring well to heat through. Transfer to a serving plate and serve immediately.

COOK'S TIP

Open up the squid rings and, using a sharp knife, score a lattice pattern on the flesh to make them look attractive.

Fried Shrimp with Cashews

Serves 4

INGREDIENTS

2 garlic cloves, crushed
1 tbsp cornstarch
pinch of superfine sugar
1 pound raw jumbo shrimp
4 tbsp vegetable oil

1 leek, sliced
4¹/2 ounces broccoli florets
1 orange bell pepper, seeded
  and diced
³/4 cup unsalted cashew nuts

SAUCE:
³/4 cup fish stock
1 tbsp cornstarch
dash of chili sauce
2 tsp sesame oil
1 tbsp Chinese rice wine

1 Mix together the garlic, cornstarch, and sugar in a large bowl. Peel and devein the jumbo shrimp. Stir the shrimp into the cornstarch mixture to coat thoroughly.

2 Heat the oil in a preheated wok and add the shrimp mixture. Stir-fry over a high heat for 20–30 seconds, until the shrimp turn pink. Remove the shrimp from the wok with a slotted spoon, drain on paper towels, and set aside.

3 Add the leek, broccoli, and bell pepper to the wok and stir-fry for 2 minutes.

4 To make the sauce, mix together the fish stock, cornstarch, chili sauce to taste, the sesame oil, and Chinese rice wine. Add the mixture to the wok, together with the cashews. Return the shrimp to the wok and cook, stirring frequently, for 1 minute to heat through completely. Transfer to a warm serving dish and serve immediately.

VARIATION

This recipe also works well with chicken, pork, or beef strips instead of the shrimp. Use 8 ounces meat instead of 1 pound shrimp.

Shrimp Fu Yong

Serves 4

INGREDIENTS

2 tbsp vegetable oil

1 carrot, peeled and grated

5 eggs, beaten

8 ounces raw small shrimp, peeled

1 tbsp light soy sauce

pinch of Chinese five-spice powder

2 scallions, chopped

2 tsp sesame seeds

1 tsp sesame oil

1 Heat the vegetable oil in a preheated wok.

2 Add the carrot and stir-fry for 1–2 minutes.

3 Push the carrot to one side of the wok and add the eggs. Cook, stirring gently, for 1–2 minutes.

4 Stir the small shrimp, soy sauce, and five-spice powder into the mixture in the wok. Stir-fry the mixture for 2–3 minutes, or until the small shrimp have changed color and the mixture is almost dry.

5 Turn the shrimp fu yong out onto a warm serving plate and sprinkle the scallions, sesame seeds, and sesame oil on top. Serve immediately.

VARIATION

For a more substantial dish, you could add 1 cup cooked long-grain rice with the small shrimp in step 4. Taste and adjust the quantities of soy sauce, Chinese five-spice powder, and sesame oil if necessary. This is a useful way of using up leftover rice.

COOK'S TIP

If only cooked shrimp are available, add them just before the end of cooking, but make sure they are fully incorporated into the fu yong. They require only heating through. Overcooking will make them chewy and tasteless.

Cantonese Shrimp

Serves 4

INGREDIENTS

5 tbsp vegetable oil

4 garlic cloves, crushed

1 1/2 pounds raw shrimp, shelled
    and deveined

2-inch piece fresh ginger root,
    chopped

6 ounces lean pork, diced

1 leek, sliced

3 eggs, beaten

shredded leek and red bell pepper
    matchsticks, to garnish

SAUCE:

2 tbsp dry sherry

2 tbsp light soy sauce

2 tsp superfine sugar

2/3 cup fish stock

4 1/2 tsp cornstarch

3 tbsp water

1 Heat 2 tablespoons of the vegetable oil in a preheated wok. Add the garlic and stir-fry for about 30 seconds. Add the shrimp and stir-fry for 5 minutes, or until they change color. Remove the shrimp from the wok with a slotted spoon, drain, set aside, and keep warm.

2 Add the remaining oil to the wok and heat. Add the ginger, diced pork, and leek and stir-fry over a medium heat for 4–5 minutes, or until the pork is lightly colored and sealed.

3 Add the sherry, soy sauce, sugar, and fish stock to the wok. Blend the cornstarch with the water to form a smooth paste and stir it into the wok. Cook, stirring, until the sauce thickens and clears.

4 Return the shrimp to the wok and add the beaten eggs. Cook for 5–6 minutes, stirring occasionally, until the eggs set. Transfer to a warm serving dish, garnish with shredded leek and bell pepper matchsticks, and serve.

COOK'S TIP

If possible, use Chinese rice wine instead of the sherry.

Squid with Oyster Sauce

Serves 4

INGREDIENTS

1 pound squid
²/3 cup vegetable oil
¹/2-inch piece fresh ginger
    root, grated

2 ounces snow peas
5 tbsp hot fish stock
red bell pepper triangles, to garnish

SAUCE:
1 tbsp oyster sauce
1 tbsp light soy sauce
pinch of superfine sugar
1 garlic clove, crushed

1 To prepare the squid, cut down the center of the body lengthwise. Flatten the squid out, inside uppermost, and score a lattice design deep into the flesh, using a sharp knife.

2 To make the sauce, combine the oyster sauce, soy sauce, sugar, and garlic in a small bowl. Stir to dissolve the sugar and set aside until required.

3 Heat the vegetable oil in a preheated wok until almost smoking.

Lower the heat slightly, add the squid, and stir-fry until they curl up. Remove with a slotted spoon and drain thoroughly on paper towels.

4 Pour off all but 2 tablespoons of the oil and return the wok to the heat. Add the ginger and snow peas and stir-fry for about 1 minute.

5 Return the squid to the wok and pour in the sauce and hot fish stock. Simmer the mixture for

about 3 minutes, or until the liquid has thickened.

6 Transfer to a warm serving dish, garnish with bell pepper triangles, and serve immediately.

COOK'S TIP

Take care not to overcook the squid, otherwise it will be rubbery and unappetizing.

Scallops in Ginger Sauce

Serves 4

INGREDIENTS

2 tbsp vegetable oil

1 pound scallops, cleaned
    and halved

1-inch piece fresh ginger root,
    finely chopped

3 garlic cloves, crushed

2 leeks, shredded

$3/4$ cup shelled peas

$4^1/2$ ounces canned bamboo
    shoots, drained and rinsed

2 tbsp light soy sauce

2 tbsp unsweetened orange juice

1 tsp superfine sugar

orange zest, to garnish

1 Heat the oil in a preheated wok. Add the scallops and stir-fry for 1–2 minutes. Remove the scallops from the wok with a slotted spoon and set aside.

2 Add the ginger and garlic to the wok and stir-fry for 30 seconds. Stir in the leeks and peas and cook, stirring, for a further 2 minutes.

3 Add the bamboo shoots and return the scallops to the wok. Stir gently to mix without breaking up the scallops.

4 Stir in the soy sauce, orange juice, and sugar and cook for 1–2 minutes. Transfer to a serving dish, garnish with the orange zest, and serve immediately.

COOK'S TIP

Frozen scallops may be thawed and used in this recipe, adding them at the end of cooking to prevent them from breaking up. If you are buying scallops already shelled, check whether they are fresh or frozen. Fresh scallops are cream colored and more translucent, while frozen scallops tend to be pure white.

Crab in Ginger Sauce

Serves 4

INGREDIENTS

2 small cooked crabs

2 tbsp vegetable oil

3-inch piece fresh ginger root, grated

2 garlic cloves, thinly sliced

1 green bell pepper, seeded and cut into thin strips

6 scallions, cut into 1-inch lengths

2 tbsp dry sherry

$1/2$ tsp sesame oil

$2/3$ cup fish stock

1 tsp light brown sugar

2 tsp cornstarch

$2/3$ cup water

1 Rinse the crabs and gently loosen around the shell at the top. Using a sharp knife, cut away the gray tissue and discard. Rinse the crabs again.

2 Twist off the legs and claws from the crabs. Using a pair of crab claw crackers or a cleaver, gently crack the claws to break through the shell to expose the flesh. Remove and discard any loose pieces of shell.

3 Separate the body and discard the inedible lungs and sac. Cut down the center of each crab to separate the body into two pieces and then cut each of these in half again.

4 Heat the oil in a preheated wok. Add the ginger and garlic and stir-fry for 1 minute. Add the crab pieces and stir-fry for 1 minute.

5 Stir in the bell pepper, scallions, sherry, sesame oil, stock, and sugar. Bring to a boil, reduce the heat, cover, and simmer for 3–4 minutes.

6 Blend the cornstarch with the water to make a smooth paste and stir it into the wok. Bring to a boil, stirring, until the sauce is thickened and clear. Transfer to a warm serving dish and serve immediately.

COOK'S TIP

If desired, remove the crab meat from the shells prior to stir-frying and add to the wok with the bell pepper.

Potato-Topped Cod

Serves 4

INGREDIENTS

1/4 cup butter	1 tsp garam masala	4 cod fillets, about 6 ounces each
4 waxy potatoes, sliced	pinch of chili powder	1/2 cup grated Swiss cheese
1 large onion, finely chopped	1 tbsp chopped fresh dill	salt and pepper
1 tsp wholegrain mustard	1 1/4 cups fresh bread crumbs	fresh dill sprigs, to garnish

1 Melt half the butter in a skillet. Add the rest potatoes and fry for 5 minutes, turning until they are browned all over. Remove the potatoes from the skillet with a slotted spoon.

2 Add the remaining butter to the skillet and stir in the onion, mustard, garam masala, chili powder, chopped dill, and bread crumbs. Cook for 1–2 minutes, stirring well.

3 Layer half the potatoes in the base of an ovenproof dish and place the cod fillets on top. Cover the cod fillets with the rest of the potato slices. Season to taste with salt and pepper.

4 Spoon the spicy mixture from the skillet over the potatoes and sprinkle with the grated Swiss cheese.

5 Cook in a preheated oven at 400°F for 20–25 minutes, or until the topping is golden and crisp and the fish is cooked through. Garnish with fresh dill sprigs and serve at once.

COOK'S TIP

This dish is ideal served with baked vegetables which can be cooked in the oven at the same time.

VARIATION

You can use any fish for this recipe: for special occasions use salmon steaks or fillets.

Seafood Stir-fry

Serves 4

INGREDIENTS

3¹/₂ ounces small, thin
    asparagus spears, trimmed
1 tbsp sunflower oil
1-inch piece fresh ginger root,
    cut into thin strips
1 medium leek, shredded
2 medium carrots, julienned

3¹/₂ ounces baby corn cobs,
    quartered lengthwise
2 tbsp light soy sauce
1 tbsp oyster sauce
1 tsp clear honey
1 pound cooked, assorted
    shellfish, thawed if frozen

freshly cooked egg noodles,
    to serve

TO GARNISH:
4 large cooked shrimp
small bunch fresh chives,
    freshly snipped

1 Bring a small pan of water to a boil and blanch the asparagus for 1–2 minutes. Drain, set aside, and keep warm.

2 Heat the oil in a wok or large skillet and stir-fry the ginger, leek, carrot, and corn for 3 minutes.

3 Add the soy sauce, oyster sauce, and honey to the wok or skillet. Stir in the shellfish and continue to stir-fry for

2–3 minutes until the vegetables are just tender and the shellfish is heated through. Add the blanched asparagus to the wok or skillet and stir-fry for about 2 minutes.

4 To serve, pile the cooked noodles onto 4 warm serving plates and spoon the seafood and vegetable stir-fry on top. Serve garnished with a large shrimp and freshly snipped chives.

COOK'S TIP

When you are preparing dense vegetables, such as carrots and other root vegetables, for stir-frying, slice them into thin, evenly sized pieces so that they cook quickly and at the same rate. Delicate vegetables, such as bell peppers, leeks, and scallions, do not need to be cut as thinly.

Citrus Fish Kabobs

Serves 4

INGREDIENTS

1 pound firm white fish fillets (such as cod or monkfish)	1 bunch fresh bay leaves	TO SERVE:
	1 tsp finely grated lemon rind	crusty bread
1 pound thick salmon fillet	3 tbsp lemon juice	mixed salad
2 large oranges	2 tsp clear honey	
1 pink grapefruit	2 garlic cloves, crushed	
	salt and pepper	

1 Skin the white fish and the salmon, rinse, and pat dry on absorbent paper towels. Cut each fillet into 16 pieces.

2 Using a sharp knife, remove the skin and pith from the oranges and grapefruit. Cut out the segments of flesh, removing all remaining traces of the pith and dividing membrane.

3 Thread the pieces of fish alternately with the orange and grapefruit segments and the bay leaves onto 8 skewers. Place the kabobs in a shallow dish.

4 Mix together the lemon rind and juice, the honey, and garlic. Pour over the kabobs and season. Cover and chill for 2 hours, turning occasionally.

5 Preheat the broiler. Remove the kabobs from the marinade and place on the rack. Cook for 7–8 minutes, turning once, until cooked through.

6 Drain the kabobs thoroughly, transfer to serving plates, and serve with crusty bread and a fresh salad.

VARIATION

This dish makes an unusual starter. Try it with any firm fish—shark or swordfish, for example—or with tuna for a meatier texture.

Five-Spice Salmon with Ginger Stir-Fry

Serves 4

INGREDIENTS

4 salmon fillets, skinned, 4 ounces each	1-inch piece fresh ginger root	TO GARNISH:
2 tsp five-spice powder	2 tbsp ginger wine	leek, shredded
1 large leek	2 tbsp light soy sauce	fresh ginger root, shredded
1 large carrot	1 tbsp vegetable oil	carrot, shredded
4 ounces snow peas	salt and pepper	

1 Wash the salmon and pat dry on absorbent paper towels. Rub the five-spice powder into both sides of the fish and season with salt and pepper to taste. Set aside until required.

2 Using a sharp knife, trim the leek, slice it down the center, and rinse under cold water to remove any dirt. Finely shred the leek. Peel the carrot and cut it into very thin strips. Top and tail the snow peas and cut them into shreds. Peel the ginger and slice thinly into strips.

3 Place all of the vegetables into a large bowl and toss in the ginger wine and 1 tablespoon of soy sauce. Set aside.

4 Preheat the broiler. Place the salmon fillets on the rack and brush with the remaining soy sauce. Cook for 2–3 minutes on each side, until completely cooked through.

5 While the salmon is cooking, heat the oil in a nonstick wok or large skillet and stir-fry the vegetables for 5 minutes, until just tender. Ensure that you do not overcook the vegetables—they should still have bite. Transfer to serving plates.

6 Drain the salmon on paper towels and serve on a bed of stir-fried vegetables. Garnish with shredded leek, ginger, and carrot and serve.

Oriental Shellfish Kabobs

Makes 12

INGREDIENTS

12 ounces raw tiger shrimp,
  peeled leaving tails intact
12 ounces scallops, cleaned,
  trimmed, and halved
  (quartered if large)
1 bunch scallions, sliced into
  1-inch pieces
1 medium red bell pepper,
  seeded and cubed

$3^1/2$ ounces baby corn cobs,
  trimmed and sliced into
  $^1/2$-inch pieces
3 tbsp dark soy sauce
$^1/2$ tsp hot chili powder
$^1/2$ tsp ground ginger
1 tbsp sunflower oil
1 red chili, seeded and sliced

DIP:
4 tbsp dark soy sauce
4 tbsp dry sherry
2 tsp clear honey
1-inch piece fresh ginger root,
  peeled and grated
1 scallion, trimmed and sliced
  very finely

1 Soak 12 wooden skewers in cold water for 10 minutes to prevent them from burning.

2 Divide the shrimp, scallops, scallions, bell pepper, and baby corn cobs into 12 portions and thread onto the cooled wooden skewers. Cover the ends with foil so that they do not burn, and place in a shallow dish.

3 Mix the soy sauce, chili powder, and ground ginger and coat the shellfish and vegetable kabobs. Cover and chill for about 2 hours.

4 Preheat the broiler. Arrange the kabobs on the rack, brush the shellfish and vegetables with oil, and cook for 2–3 minutes on each side, until the shrimp turn pink, the scallops become opaque, and the vegetables are soft.

5 Mix together the dip ingredients and set aside.

6 Remove the foil and transfer the kabobs to a warm serving platter. Garnish with sliced chili and serve with the dip.

Tuna Steaks with Fragrant Spices & Lime

Serves 4

INGREDIENTS

4 tuna steaks, 6 ounces each
1/2 tsp finely grated lime rind
1 garlic clove, crushed
2 tsp olive oil

1 tsp ground cumin
1 tsp ground coriander
pepper
1 tbsp lime juice
fresh cilantro, to garnish

TO SERVE:
avocado relish (see Cook's Tip)
lime wedges
tomato wedges

1 Trim the skin from the tuna steaks, rinse, and pat dry on absorbent paper towels.

2 In a small bowl, mix together the lime rind, garlic, olive oil, cumin, ground coriander, and pepper to make a paste.

3 Spread the paste thinly on both sides of the tuna. Heat a nonstick, ridged skillet until hot and press the tuna steaks into the pan to seal them.

Lower the heat and cook for 5 minutes. Turn the fish over and cook for a further 4–5 minutes, until the fish is cooked through. Drain on absorbent paper towels and transfer to a warm serving plate.

4 Sprinkle the lime juice and chopped cilantro over the fish.

5 Serve with freshly made avocado relish (see Cook's Tip), lime wedges and tomato wedges.

COOK'S TIP

For low-fat avocado relish to serve with tuna, peel and remove the pit from one small ripe avocado. Toss in 1 tbsp lime juice. Mix in 1 tbsp freshly chopped cilantro and 1 small finely chopped red onion. Stir in some chopped fresh mango or a chopped medium tomato and season with salt and pepper to taste.

Teriyaki Stir-Fried Salmon with Crispy Leeks

Serves 4

INGREDIENTS

1 pound salmon fillet, skinned	1 tsp rice wine vinegar	4 tbsp corn oil
2 tbsp sweet soy sauce	1 tbsp sugar	1 leek, thinly shredded
2 tbsp tomato ketchup	1 clove garlic, crushed	finely chopped red chilies, to garnish

1 Using a sharp knife, cut the salmon into slices. Place the slices of salmon in a shallow nonmetallic dish.

2 Mix together the soy sauce, tomato ketchup, rice wine vinegar, sugar, and garlic.

3 Pour the mixture over the salmon, toss well, and marinate for about 30 minutes.

4 Meanwhile, heat 3 tablespoons of the corn oil in a large preheated wok.

5 Add the leeks to the wok and stir-fry over a medium high heat for about 10 minutes, or until the leeks become crispy and tender.

6 Using a slotted spoon, carefully remove the leeks from the wok and transfer to warm serving plates.

7 Add the remaining oil to the wok. Add the salmon and the marinade to the wok and cook for 2 minutes. Spoon it over the leeks, garnish, and serve immediately.

VARIATION

You can use a fillet of beef instead of the salmon, if wished.

Stir-Fried Salmon with Pineapple

Serves 4

INGREDIENTS

1 cup baby corn cobs, halved	1 green bell pepper, seeded and sliced	½ cup bean sprouts
2 tbsp sunflower oil	1 pound salmon fillet, skin removed	2 tbsp tomato ketchup
1 red onion, sliced	1 tbsp paprika	2 tbsp soy sauce
1 orange bell pepper, seeded and sliced	8 ounce can cubed pineapple, drained	2 tbsp medium sherry
		1 tsp cornstarch

1 Using a sharp knife, cut the baby corn cobs in half.

2 Heat the sunflower oil in a large preheated wok. Add the onion, bell peppers, and baby corn cobs to the wok and stir-fry for 5 minutes.

3 Rinse the salmon fillet under cold running water and pat dry with absorbent paper towels.

4 Cut the salmon flesh into thin strips and place in a large bowl. Sprinkle with the paprika and toss until well coated.

5 Add the salmon to the wok, together with the pineapple, and stir-fry for a further 2–3 minutes or until the fish is tender.

6 Add the bean sprouts to the wok and toss well.

7 Mix together the tomato ketchup, soy sauce, sherry, and cornstarch. Add the mixture to the wok and cook until the juices thicken.

Transfer to warm serving plates and serve immediately.

VARIATION

You can use trout fillets instead of the salmon as an alternative, if wished.

Stir-Fried Cod with Mango

Serves 4

INGREDIENTS

2–3 medium carrots	1 green bell pepper, seeded and sliced	1 tbsp soy sauce
2 tbsp vegetable oil	1 pound skinless cod fillet	1 ¹/₃ cup tropical fruit juice
1 red onion, sliced	1 ripe mango	1 tbsp lime juice
1 red bell pepper, seeded and sliced	1 tsp cornstarch	1 tbsp chopped cilantro

1 Using a sharp knife, slice the carrots into thin sticks.

2 Heat the vegetable oil in a preheated wok.

3 Add the onions, carrots, and bell peppers to the wok and stir-fry for 5 minutes.

4 Using a sharp knife, cut the cod into small cubes.

5 Peel the mango, then carefully remove the flesh from the central pit. Cut the flesh into thin slices.

6 Add the cod and mango to the wok and stir-fry for a further 4–5 minutes, or until the fish is cooked through. Do not stir the mixture too much or you may break the fish up.

7 Mix the cornstarch, soy sauce, fruit juice, and lime juice in a small bowl.

8 Pour the cornstarch mixture over the stir-fry and allow the mixture to bubble and the juices to thicken. Scatter with cilantro, transfer to a warm serving dish, and serve immediately.

VARIATION

You can use papaya as an alternative to the mango, if wished.

Stir-Fried Gingered Monkfish

Serves 4

INGREDIENTS

1 pound monkfish	1 tbsp corn oil	3 scallions, sliced
1 tbsp freshly grated ginger root	1 cup fine asparagus	1 tsp sesame oil
2 tbsp sweet chili sauce		

1 Remove the membrane from the monkfish, then using a sharp knife, slice the flesh into thin flat rounds.

2 Mix the ginger with the chili sauce in a small bowl.

3 Brush the ginger and chili sauce mixture over the monkfish pieces.

4 Heat the corn oil in a large preheated wok.

5 Add the monkfish, asparagus, and scallions to the wok and stir-fry for about 5 minutes.

6 Remove the wok from the heat, drizzle the sesame oil over the stir-fry, and toss well to combine.

7 Transfer to warm serving plates and serve immediately.

VARIATION

Monkfish is quite expensive, but it is well worth using as it has a wonderful flavor and texture. Otherwise, could use cubes of chunky cod fillet instead.

COOK'S TIP

Some recipes specify to grate ginger before it is cooked with other ingredients. To do this, just peel the flesh and rub it at a 45 degree angle up and down on the fine section of a metal grater, or use a special wooden or ceramic ginger grater.

Fried Fish with Coconut & Basil

Serves 4

INGREDIENTS

2 tbsp vegetable oil
450 g/1 lb skinless cod fillet
25 g/1 oz/¼ cup seasoned flour
1 clove garlic, crushed

2 tbsp red Thai curry paste
1 tbsp fish sauce
300 ml/½ pint/1¼ cups coconut milk
175 g/6 oz cherry tomatoes, halved

20 fresh basil leaves
fragrant rice, to serve

1 Heat the vegetable oil in a large preheated wok.

2 Using a sharp knife, cut the fish into large cubes, taking care to remove any bones with a pair of tweezers.

3 Place the seasoned flour in a bowl. Add the cubes of fish and mix until well coated.

4 Add the coated fish to the wok and stir-fry over a high heat for 3–4 minutes, or until the fish just begins to brown at the edges.

5 Mix together the garlic, curry paste, fish sauce, and coconut milk in a bowl. Pour the mixture over the fish and bring to a boil.

6 Add the tomatoes to the mixture in the wok and simmer for 5 minutes.

7 Roughly chop or tear the fresh basil leaves. Add the basil to the wok, stir carefully to combine, taking care not to break up the cubes of fish.

8 Transfer to serving plates and serve hot with fragrant rice.

COOK'S TIP

Take care not to overcook the dish once the tomatoes are added, otherwise they will break down and the skins will come away.

Shrimp Omelet

Serves 4

INGREDIENTS

2 tbsp sunflower oil
4 scallions, sliced
12 ounces peeled shrimp

½ cup bean sprouts
1 tsp cornstarch

1 tbsp light soy sauce
6 eggs

1 Heat the sunflower oil in a large preheated wok.

2 Using a sharp knife, trim the scallions and cut them into thin slices.

3 Add the shrimp, scallions, and bean sprouts to the wok and stir-fry for 2 minutes.

4 Mix together the cornstarch and soy sauce in a small bowl.

5 Beat together the eggs and 3 tablespoons of cold water and then blend with the cornstarch and soy mixture.

6 Add the egg mixture to the wok and cook for about 5–6 minutes, or until the mixture is just setting.

7 Transfer the omelet to a serving plate and cut into quarters to serve.

COOK'S TIP

It is important to use fresh bean sprouts for this dish as the canned ones don't have the crunchy texture necessary.

VARIATION

Add any other vegetables of your choice, such as grated carrot or cooked peas, to the omelet in step 3, if you wish.

Chinese Cabbage with Shiitake Mushrooms & Crab Meat

Serves 4

INGREDIENTS

8 ounces shiitake mushrooms
2 tbsp vegetable oil
2 cloves garlic, crushed

6 scallions, sliced
1 head Chinese cabbage, shredded
1 tbsp mild curry paste

6 tbsp coconut milk
7 ounce can white crab meat, drained
1 tsp chili flakes

1 Using a sharp knife, cut the the mushrooms into slices.

2 Heat the vegetable oil in a large preheated wok.

3 Add the mushrooms and garlic to the wok and stir-fry for 3 minutes, or until the mushrooms have softened.

4 Add the scallions and shredded Chinese cabbage to the wok and stir-fry until the leaves have wilted.

5 Mix together the mild curry paste and coconut milk in a small bowl.

6 Add the curry paste and coconut milk mixture to the wok, together with the crab meat and chili flakes. Mix together until thoroughly combined and heat through until the juices start to bubble.

7 Transfer to warm serving bowls and then serve immediately.

COOK'S TIP

Shiitake mushrooms are now readily available in the fresh vegetable section of most large supermarkets.

Seared Scallops with Butter Sauce

Serves 4

INGREDIENTS

1 pound scallops, without corals	2 tbsp vegetable oil	3 tbsp sweet soy sauce
6 scallions	1 green chili, seeded and sliced	2 tbsp butter, diced

1 Rinse the scallops well under cold running water, then pat the scallops dry with absorbent paper towels.

2 Using a sharp knife, slice each scallop in half horizontally.

3 Using a sharp knife, trim and thinly slice the scallions.

4 Heat the vegetable oil in a large preheated wok.

5 Add the sliced chili, scallions, and scallops to the wok and stir-fry over a high heat for about 4–5 minutes, or until the scallops are just cooked through and have become slightly opaque.

6 Add the soy sauce and butter to the scallop stir-fry and heat through until the butter melts.

COOK'S TIP

If you buy scallops on the shell, slide a knife underneath the membrane to loosen and cut off the tough muscle that holds the scallop to the shell. Discard the black stomach sac and intestinal vein.

COOK'S TIP

Use frozen scallops if desired, but make sure they are completely thawed before cooking. In addition, do not overcook them, as they will easily disintegrate.

7 Transfer to warm serving bowls and serve hot.

Stir-Fried Squid with Green Bell Peppers & Black Bean Sauce

Serves 4

INGREDIENTS

1 pound squid rings	1 green bell pepper	1 red onion, sliced
2 tbsp all-purpose flour	2 tbsp peanut oil	5¾ ounce jar black bean sauce
½ tsp salt		

1 Rinse the squid rings under cold running water and pat dry with absorbent paper towels.

2 Place the all-purpose flour and salt in a bowl and mix together. Add the squid rings and toss until they are finely coated.

3 Using a sharp knife, seed the bell pepper. Slice the bell pepper into thin strips.

4 Heat the peanut oil in a large preheated wok.

5 Add the bell pepper and red onion to the wok and stir-fry for about 2 minutes, or until the vegetables are just beginning to soften.

6 Add the squid rings to the wok and cook for a further 5 minutes, or until the squid is cooked through.

7 Add the black bean sauce to the wok and heat through until the juices are bubbling. Transfer to warm serving bowls and serve immediately.

COOK'S TIP

Serve this recipe with fried rice or noodles tossed in soy sauce, if you wish.

Shrimp with Bell Peppers

Serves 4

INGREDIENTS

1 pound frozen shrimp	1 tsp crushed garlic	1 medium red bell pepper
¹/₂ bunch fresh cilantro leaves	1 tsp salt	6 tbsp sweet butter
	1 medium green bell pepper, sliced	

1 Defrost the shrimp and rinse under cold running water twice. Drain the shrimp thoroughly and place in a large mixing bowl.

2 Using a sharp knife, finely chop the bunch of fresh cilantro.

3 Add the garlic, salt, and fresh cilantro leaves to the shrimp and set aside until required.

4 Core and seed the bell peppers and cut the flesh into thin slices, using a sharp knife.

5 Melt the butter in a large skillet. Add the shrimp to the pan and stir-fry, stirring and tossing the shrimp gently, for 10–12 minutes.

6 Add the bell peppers to the pan and cook for a further 3–5 minutes, stirring occasionally.

7 Transfer the shrimp and bell pepper to a serving dish and serve hot.

VARIATION

You could use large jumbo shrimp in this dish, if desired.

Shrimp with Tomatoes

Serves 4-6

INGREDIENTS

3 medium onions	1 tsp crushed garlic	12 ounces frozen shrimp
1 green bell pepper	1 tsp salt	3 tbsp oil
1 tsp finely chopped fresh	1 tsp chili powder	14 ounce can tomatoes
ginger root	2 tbsp lemon juice	fresh cilantro leaves,
		to garnish

1 Using a sharp knife, slice the onions and the green bell pepper.

2 Place the ginger, garlic, salt, and chili powder in a small bowl and mix to combine. Add the lemon juice and mix to form a paste.

3 Place the shrimp in a bowl of cold water and set aside to thaw. Drain thoroughly.

4 Heat the oil in a medium-size saucepan. Add the onions and sauté until golden brown.

5 Add the spice paste to the onions, reduce the heat to low, and cook, stirring and mixing well, for about 3 minutes.

6 Add the tomatoes, tomato juice, and the green bell pepper, and cook for 5-7 minutes, stirring occasionally.

7 Add the shrimp to the pan and cook for 10 minutes, stirring occasionally.

8 Garnish with fresh cilantro leaves and serve hot with boiled rice and crisp salad greens.

COOK'S TIP

Fresh ginger root looks rather like a knobby potato. The skin should be peeled, then the flesh grated, finely chopped, or sliced. Ginger is also available ground: this can be used as a substitute for fresh ginger root, but the fresh root is far superior.

Bacon & Scallop Skewers

Makes 4

INGREDIENTS

grated rind and juice of $^1/_2$
   lemon
4 tbsp sunflower oil
$^1/_2$ tsp dried dill

12 scallops
1 red bell pepper
1 green bell pepper

1 yellow bell pepper
6 slices bacon

1 Mix together the lemon rind and juice, sunflower oil, and dried dill in a nonmetallic dish. Add the scallops and mix thoroughly to coat in the marinade. Marinate for 1–2 hours in the refrigerator.

2 Cut the red, green, and yellow bell peppers in half and seed them. Cut the bell pepper halves into 1-inch pieces and then set aside in a small bowl until required.

3 Carefully stretch the bacon slices with the back of a knife blade, then cut each bacon slice in half.

4 Remove the scallops from the marinade, reserving any excess marinade. Wrap a piece of bacon around each scallop.

5 Thread the bacon-wrapped scallops onto skewers, alternating with the bell pepper pieces.

6 Broil the bacon and scallop skewers over hot coals for about 5 minutes, basting frequently with the lemon and oil marinade.

7 Transfer the bacon and scallop skewers to serving plates and serve at once.

VARIATION

Peel 4–8 raw shrimp and add them to the marinade with the scallops. Thread them onto the skewers alternately with the scallops and bell peppers.

Caribbean Shrimp

Serves 4

INGREDIENTS

16 cooked tiger shrimp
1 small pineapple
flaked coconut, to garnish
   (optional)

MARINADE:
$2/3$ cup pineapple juice
2 tbsp white wine vinegar
2 tbsp dark brown sugar
2 tbsp shredded coconut

1 Peel the shrimp, leaving the tails attached if preferred.

2 Peel the pineapple and cut it in half lengthwise. Cut one pineapple half into wedges, then into chunks.

3 To make the marinade, mix together half of the pineapple juice and the vinegar, sugar, and coconut in a shallow, nonmetallic dish. Add the peeled shrimp and pineapple chunks and toss until well coated. Marinate for at least 30 minutes in the refrigerator.

4 Remove the pineapple and shrimp from the marinade and thread them onto skewers. Reserve the marinade.

5 Strain the marinade and place in a food processor. Roughly chop the remaining pineapple and add to the processor with the remaining pineapple juice. Process the pineapple for a few seconds in order to produce a thick sauce.

6 Pour the sauce into a small saucepan. Bring to a boil, then simmer for about 5 minutes. This can be done by the side of the barbecue if preferred.

7 Transfer the kabobs to the barbecue and brush with some of the sauce. Broil for about 5 minutes until the kabobs are piping hot. Turn the kabobs, brushing occasionally with the sauce. Serve with extra sauce, sprinkled with flaked coconut (if using), on the side.

Herb & Garlic Shrimp

Serves 4

INGREDIENTS

12 ounces raw shrimp, peeled	4 tbsp lemon juice	2 cloves garlic, chopped
2 tbsp chopped, fresh parsley	2 tbsp olive oil	salt and pepper
	5 tbsp butter	

1 Place the prepared shrimp in a shallow, nonmetallic dish with the parsley, lemon juice, and salt and pepper to taste. Stir gently to mix. Marinate the shrimp in the herb mixture for at least 30 minutes in the refrigerator.

2 Heat the oil and butter in a small pan, together with the garlic, until the butter melts. Stir to mix thoroughly.

3 Remove the shrimp from the marinade with a slotted spoon and add them to the pan containing the garlic butter.

Stir the shrimp into the garlic butter until well coated all over, then thread the shrimp onto several skewers.

4 Broil the kabobs over hot coals for 5–10 minutes, turning the skewers occasionally, until the shrimp turn pink and are cooked through. Generously brush the shrimp with the remaining garlic butter during the cooking time.

5 Transfer the herb and garlic shrimp kabobs to warm serving plates. Drizzle over any of the remaining garlic butter and serve at once.

VARIATION

If raw shrimp are unavailable, use cooked shrimp, but reduce the cooking time. Small cooked shrimp can also be cooked in a foil packet instead of on the skewers. Marinate and toss the cooked shrimp in the garlic butter, wrap in foil, and cook for about 5 minutes, shaking the packets once or twice.

Desserts & Puddings

For many people the favorite part of any meal, the desserts and puddings that have been selected here will be a treat for all palates. Whether you are a chocolate-lover or are on a diet, there is a recipe here to tempt you. Choose from a light summer delicacy or a hearty hot winter treat; you will find desserts to indulge in all year round. If you are looking for a chilled sweet, choose the Granita or rich Vanilla Ice Cream, or if a warm pudding takes your fancy, Baked Bananas or Pan-Cooked Apples in Red Wine will do the trick.

If you are after a low-fat dessert, fresh fruit is the ideal way to finish off your meal. Fruit contains no fat and is naturally sweet and full of vitamins. However, if you are looking for a special treat for the children's lunch box, choose from No-Cook Fruit and Nut Chocolate Fudge or Nutty Chocolate Clusters. All of the recipes are easy to prepare and are packed full of flavor.

Chocolate Banana Sundae

Serves 4

INGREDIENTS

GLOSSY CHOCOLATE SAUCE:
2 ounces dark chocolate
4 tbsp light corn syrup
1 tbsp butter
1 tbsp brandy or rum (optional)

SUNDAE:
4 bananas
$^2/_3$ cup heavy cream
8–12 scoops of good quality vanilla
  ice cream

$^3/_4$ cup slivered or chopped
  almonds, toasted
grated or flaked chocolate,
  to sprinkle
4 fan wafer cookies

1 To make chocolate sauce, break the chocolate into small pieces and place in a double boiler with the syrup and butter. Heat until melted, stirring until well combined. Remove the bowl from the heat and stir in the brandy or rum, if using.

2 Slice the bananas and whip the cream until just holding its shape. Place a scoop of ice cream in the bottom of 4 tall sundae dishes. Top with slices of banana, chocolate sauce, cream, and a sprinkling of nuts.

3 Repeat the layers, finishing with a spoonful of cream, sprinkled with nuts and a little grated or flaked chocolate. Serve with fan wafer cookies.

VARIATION

Use half vanilla ice cream and half chocolate ice cream, if desired.

VARIATION

For a traditional banana split, halve the bananas lengthwise and place on a plate with two scoops of ice cream between. Top with cream and sprinkle with nuts. Serve with the glossy chocolate sauce poured over the top.

Black Forest Trifle

Serves 6–8

INGREDIENTS

6 thin slices chocolate butter
  cream roll
2 x 14 ounce cans black cherries
2 tbsp kirsch
1 tbsp cornstarch
2 tbsp superfine sugar

1¾ cups milk
3 egg yolks
1 egg
2¾ ounces dark chocolate
1¼ cups heavy cream,
  lightly whipped

TO DECORATE:
dark chocolate, melted
maraschino cherries (optional)

1 Place the slices of chocolate roll in the bottom of a glass bowl.

2 Drain the black cherries, reserving 6 tablespoons of the juice. Arrange the cherries on top of the layer of cake. Sprinkle with the reserved cherry juice and the kirsch.

3 In a bowl, mix the cornstarch and super-fine sugar. Stir in enough of the milk to mix to a smooth paste. Beat in the egg yolks and the whole egg.

4 Heat the remaining milk in a small saucepan until almost boiling, then gradually pour it into the egg mixture, beating until it is combined.

5 Place the bowl over a pan of hot water and cook over a low heat, stirring constantly, until the custard thickens. Add the chocolate and stir until melted.

6 Pour the chocolate custard over the cherries and cool. When cold, spread the cream over the custard, swirling with the back of a spoon. Chill before decorating.

7 To make chocolate caraque, spread the melted dark chocolate on a marble or acrylic board. As it begins to set, pull a knife through the chocolate at a 45-degree angle, working quickly. Remove each caraque as you make it and chill firmly before using.

Raspberry Shortcake

Serves 8

INGREDIENTS

1¹/₂ cups self-rising flour
7 tbsp butter, cut into cubes
¹/₃ cup superfine sugar

1 egg yolk
1 tbsp rose water
2¹/₂ cups whipping cream,
   whipped lightly
1¹/₃ cups raspberries, plus a
   few for decoration

TO DECORATE:
confectioners' sugar
mint leaves

1 Lightly grease 2 cookie sheets.

2 To make the shortcakes, sift the flour into a bowl.

3 Rub the butter into the flour with your fingers until the mixture resembles breadcrumbs.

4 Stir the sugar, egg yolk, and rose water into the mixture and bring together with your fingertips to form a soft dough. Divide the dough in half.

5 Roll each piece of dough to an 8-inch round and place each one onto a prepared cookie sheet. Crimp the edges of the dough.

6 Bake in a preheated oven at 375°F for 15 minutes, until lightly golden. Transfer the shortcakes to a wire rack and let cool.

7 Mix the cream with the raspberries and spoon on top of one of the shortcake rounds. Top with the other shortcake round, dust with a little confectioners' sugar, and decorate with the extra raspberries and mint leaves.

COOK'S TIP

The shortcake can be made a few days in advance and stored in an airtight container until required.

One Roll Fruit Pie

Serves 8

INGREDIENTS

PIE DOUGH:
1 1/2 cups all-purpose flour
7 tbsp butter, cut into
    small pieces
1 tbsp water
1 egg, separated

sugar cubes, crushed, for
    sprinkling

FILLING:
1 1/2 pound prepared fruit
    (rhubarb, gooseberries,
    plums, damsons)

6 tbsp light brown sugar
1 tbsp ground ginger

1 Thoroughly grease a large cookie sheet with a little butter.

2 To make the pie dough, place the flour and butter in a mixing bowl and rub in the butter with your fingers. Add the water and work the mixture together until a soft pie dough has formed. Wrap and chill for 30 minutes.

3 Roll out the chilled pie dough to a round measuring about 14 inches in diameter.

4 Transfer the round to the center of the greased cookie sheet. Brush the pie dough with the egg yolk.

5 To make the filling, mix the prepared fruit with the brown sugar and ground ginger and pile it into the center of the pie dough.

6 Turn in the edges of the pie dough all the way around. Brush the surface of the pie dough with the egg white and sprinkle evenly with the crushed sugar cubes.

7 Bake in a preheated oven at 400°F for 35 minutes, or until golden brown. Serve warm.

Syrup Tart

Serves 8

INGREDIENTS

9 ounces fresh ready-made
   shortcrust pie dough
1 cup light corn syrup
2 cups fresh white
   breadcrumbs
$^1/_2$ cup heavy cream

finely grated rind of $^1/_2$ lemon
   or orange
2 tbsp lemon or orange juice
custard, to serve

1 Roll out the pie dough to line an 8-inch loose-bottomed quiche pan, reserving the pie dough trimmings. Prick the base of the pie dough with a fork and chill in the refrigerator.

2 Cut out small shapes from the reserved pie dough trimmings, such as leaves, stars, or hearts, to decorate the top of the syrup tart.

3 In a mixing bowl, mix together the corn syrup, breadcrumbs, cream, grated lemon or orange rind, and lemon or orange juice.

4 Pour the mixture into the pie shell and decorate the edges of the tart with the pie dough cut-outs.

5 Bake in a preheated oven at 375°F for 35–40 minutes, or until the filling is just set.

6 Leave the tart to cool slightly in the pan for about 10–15 minutes, then turn out and serve the tart accompanied by custard.

VARIATION

Use the pie dough trimmings to create a lattice pattern on top of the tart, if preferred.

Pear Tarts

Makes 6

INGREDIENTS

9 ounces fresh ready-made
   puff pastry
8 tsp light brown sugar

2 tbsp butter (plus extra
   for brushing)
1 tbsp finely chopped
   preserved ginger

3 pears, peeled, halved, and
   cored
cream, to serve

1 On a lightly floured surface, roll out the dough. Cut out six rounds 4 inches in diameter

2 Place the rounds on a large cookie sheet and chill in the refrigerator for 30 minutes.

3 Cream together the brown sugar and butter in a small bowl, then stir in the chopped preserved ginger.

4 Prick the pastry rounds all over with a fork and spread a little of the ginger mixture onto each one.

5 Slice the pears halves lengthwise, keeping the pears intact at the tip. Carefully fan out the slices slightly.

6 Place a fanned-out pear half on top of each dough round. Make small flutes around the edge of the dough rounds and generously brush each pear half with melted butter.

7 Bake in a preheated oven at 400°F for 15–20 minutes, until the pastry is well risen and golden in color. Serve warm with a little cream.

COOK'S TIP

If you prefer, serve these tarts with vanilla ice cream for a delicious dessert.

Orange & Grapefruit Salad

Serves 4

INGREDIENTS

2 grapefruit, pink or plain
4 oranges
pared rind and juice of 1 lime

4 tbsp clear honey
2 tbsp warm water

1 sprig mint, roughly chopped
1/2 cup chopped walnuts

1 Using a sharp knife, slice the top and bottom from the grapefruit, then slice away the rest of the skin and pith.

2 Cut between each segment of the grapefruit to remove the fleshy part only.

3 Using a sharp knife, slice the top and bottom from the oranges, then slice away the rest of the skin and pith.

4 Cut between each segment of the oranges to remove the fleshy part. Add to the grapefruit.

5 Place the lime rind, 2 tablespoons of lime juice, the honey, and the warm water in a small bowl. Beat with a fork to mix the dressing.

6 Pour the dressing over the segmented fruit, add the chopped mint, and mix well. Chill in the refrigerator for 2 hours for the flavors to mingle.

7 Place the chopped walnuts on a cookie sheet. Lightly toast the walnuts under a preheated broiler for 2–3 minutes, until golden brown.

8 Sprinkle the toasted walnuts over the fruit and serve.

VARIATION

Instead of the walnuts, you could sprinkle toasted almonds, cashews, hazelnuts, or pecans over the fruit, if you prefer.

Zabaglione

Serves 4

INGREDIENTS

5 egg yolks 1/2 cup superfine sugar	2/3 cup Marsala or sweet sherry	fresh fruit or amaretti cookies, to serve (optional)

1 Place the egg yolks in a large mixing bowl.

2 Add the superfine sugar to the egg yolks and beat well until the mixture is thick and very pale and has doubled in volume.

3 Place the bowl containing the egg yolk and sugar mixture over a saucepan of gently simmering water.

4 Add the Marsala or sherry to the egg yolk and sugar mixture and continue beating until the foam mixture becomes warm. This process may take as long as 10 minutes.

5 Pour the mixture, which should be frothy and light, into 4 wine glasses.

6 Serve the zabaglione warm with fresh fruit or amaretti cookies if you wish.

VARIATION

Any other type of liqueur may be used instead of the Marsala or sweet sherry, if you prefer. Serve soft fruits, such as strawberries or raspberries, with the zabaglione—it's a delicious combination!

VARIATION

Iced or Semifreddo Zabaglione can be made by following the method here, then continuing to beat the foam while standing the bowl in cold water. Beat 2/3 cup heavy cream until it just holds its shape. Fold into the foam and freeze for about 2 hours, until just frozen.

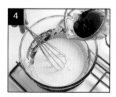

Sweet Mascarpone Mousse

Serves 4

INGREDIENTS

2 cups mascarpone cheese	14 ounces frozen summer fruits, such	red currants, to garnish
½ cup superfine sugar	as raspberries and	amaretti cookies, to serve
4 egg yolks	red currants	

1 Place the mascarpone cheese in a large mixing bowl. Using a wooden spoon, beat the mascarpone cheese until very smooth.

2 Stir the egg yolks and sugar into the mascarpone cheese, mixing well. Chill in the refrigerator for about 1 hour.

3 Spoon a layer of the mascarpone mixture into the bottom of 4 individual serving dishes. Spoon a layer of the summer fruits on top. Repeat the layers in the same order, reserving some of the mascarpone mixture for the top.

4 Chill the mousses in the refrigerator for about 20 minutes. The fruits should still be slightly frozen.

5 Serve the mascarpone mousses along with amaretti cookies.

VARIATION

Try adding 3 tablespoons of your favorite liqueur to the mascarpone cheese mixture in step 1, if desired.

COOK'S TIP

Mascarpone (sometimes spelled mascherpone) is a soft, creamy cheese from Italy. It is becoming increasingly available, and you should have no difficulty finding it in your local supermarket, or Italian delicatessen.

Rich Chocolate Loaf

Makes 16 Slices

INGREDIENTS

5¹/₂ ounces dark chocolate

6 tbsp sweet butter

7¹/₄ ounce can condensed milk

2 tsp cinnamon

¹/₂ cup almonds,

1 cup broken amaretti cookies

¹/₄ cup chopped dried no-need-to-
soak apricots

1 Line a 1½-pound loaf pan with a sheet of foil.

2 Using a very sharp knife, roughly chop the almonds.

3 Place the chocolate, butter, milk, and cinnamon in a heavy-based saucepan. Heat gently over a low heat for 3–4 minutes, stirring with a wooden spoon, until the chocolate has melted. Beat the mixture well.

4 Add the almonds, cookies, and apricots to the mixture in the saucepan, stirring with a

wooden spoon, until well mixed.

5 Pour the mixture into the prepared pan and chill in the refrigerator for about 1 hour, or until set.

6 Cut the rich chocolate loaf into slices to serve.

COOK'S TIP

To melt chocolate, first break it into manageable pieces. The smaller the pieces, the quicker it will melt.

COOK'S TIP

When baking or cooking with fat, butter has the finest flavor. If possible, it is best to use sweet butter as an ingredient in puddings and desserts, unless stated otherwise in the recipe. Reduced fat spreads are not suitable for cooking.

Peaches in White Wine

Serves 4

INGREDIENTS

4 large ripe peaches 2 tbsp confectioner's sugar, sifted	pared rind and juice of 1 orange	¾ cup medium or sweet white wine, chilled

1 Using a sharp knife, halve the peaches, remove the pits, and discard them. Peel the peaches, if desired. Slice the peaches into thin wedges.

2 Place the peach wedges in a glass serving bowl and sprinkle the sugar over them.

3 Using a sharp knife, pare the rind from the orange. Cut the orange rind into matchsticks, place them in a bowl of cold water, and set aside.

4 Squeeze the juice from the orange and pour it over the peaches, together with the wine.

5 Marinate the peaches in the refrigerator for at least 1 hour.

6 Remove the orange rind from the cold water and pat dry with paper towels.

7 Garnish the peaches with the strips of orange rind and serve immediately.

COOK'S TIP

The best way to pare the rind thinly from citrus fruits is to use a potato peeler.

COOK'S TIP

There is absolutely no need to use expensive wine in this recipe, so it can be quite economical to make.

Vanilla Ice Cream

Serves 4–6

INGREDIENTS

2¹/₂ cups heavy cream	pared rind of 1 lemon	2 egg, yolks
1 vanilla bean	4 eggs, beaten	⁷/₈ cup superfine sugar

1 Place the cream in a heavy-based saucepan and heat gently, beating. Add the vanilla bean, lemon rind, eggs, and egg yolks and heat until the mixture reaches just below boiling point.

2 Reduce the heat and cook for 8–10 minutes, beating the mixture continuously, until it has thickened.

3 Stir the sugar into the cream mixture and set aside to cool.

4 Strain the cream mixture through a fine strainer.

5 Slit open the vanilla bean, scoop out the tiny black seeds, and stir them into the cream.

6 Pour the mixture into a shallow freezing container with a lid and freeze overnight, until set. Serve when required.

COOK'S TIP

Ice cream is one of the traditional dishes of Italy. Everyone eats it and there are numerous gelato *stalls selling a wide variety of flavors, usually in a cone. It is also served in scoops and sliced.*

COOK'S TIP

To make tutti frutti ice cream, soak ²/₃ cup mixed dried fruit, such as golden raisins, cherries, apricots, candied peel, and pineapple, in 2 tablespoons Marsala or sweet sherry for 20 minutes. Follow the method for vanilla ice cream, omitting the vanilla bean, and stir in the Marsala or sherry-soaked fruit in step 5, just before freezing.

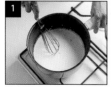

Granita

Serves 4

INGREDIENTS

LEMON GRANITA:
3 lemons
3/4 cup lemon juice
1/2 cup superfine sugar
2 1/4 cups cold water

COFFEE GRANITA:
2 tbsp instant coffee
2 tbsp sugar

2 tbsp hot water
2 1/2 cups cold water
2 tbsp rum or brandy

1 To make lemon granita, finely grate the lemon rind. Place the lemon rind, juice, and superfine sugar in a pan. Bring the mixture to a boil and simmer for 5-6 minutes, or until thick and syrupy. Let cool.

2 Once cooled, stir in the cold water and pour into a shallow freezer container with a lid. Freeze the granita for 4–5 hours, stirring occasionally to break up the ice. Serve as a palate cleanser between dinner courses.

3 To make coffee granita, place the coffee and sugar in a bowl and pour in the hot water, stirring until dissolved.

4 Stir in the cold water and rum or brandy.

5 Pour the mixture into a shallow freezer container with a lid. Freeze the granita for at least 6 hours, stirring every 1–2 hours in order to create a grainy texture. Serve with cream after dinner, if desired.

COOK'S TIP

If you would prefer a nonalcoholic version of the coffee granita, simply omit the rum or brandy and add extra instant coffee instead.

Almond Trifles

Serves 4

INGREDIENTS

8 Amaretti di Saronno cookies
4 tbsp brandy or Amaretto
   liqueur
8 ounces raspberries

1¼ cups low-fat custard
1¼ cups low-fat
   unsweetened yogurt
1 tsp almond extract

½ ounce toasted
   almonds, slivered
1 tsp cocoa powder

1 Using the end of a rolling pin, carefully crush the cookies into small pieces.

2 Divide the crushed cookies among 4 serving glasses. Sprinkle in the brandy or liqueur and let stand for about 30 minutes to allow the cookies to soften.

3 Top the layer of cookies with a layer of raspberries, reserving a few raspberries for decoration, and spoon over enough custard to just cover.

4 Mix the unsweetened yogurt with the almond extract and spoon over the custard. Chill in the refrigerator for about 30 minutes.

5 Just before serving, sprinkle with the toasted slivered almonds and dust with a little cocoa powder. Decorate with the reserved raspberries and serve at once.

VARIATION

Try this trifle with assorted summer fruits. If they are a frozen mix, use them frozen and allow them to thaw so that the juices soak into the cookie base—it will taste delicious.

Red Fruits with Foaming Sauce

Serves 4

INGREDIENTS

8 ounces redcurrants, washed
  and trimmed, thawed if
  frozen
8 ounces cranberries
3 ounces light brown sugar

³/4 cup unsweetened apple
  juice
1 cinnamon stick, broken
10¹/2 ounces small
  strawberries, washed,
  hulled, and halved

SAUCE:
8 ounces raspberries, thawed
  if frozen
2 tbsp fruit cordial
3¹/2 ounces marshmallows

1 Place the redcurrants, cranberries, and sugar in a saucepan. Pour in the apple juice and add the cinnamon stick. Bring the mixture to a boil and simmer gently for 10 minutes, until the fruit has just softened.

2 Stir the strawberries into the cranberry and sugar mixture and mix well. Transfer the mixture to a bowl, cover, and chill in the refrigerator for about 1 hour. Remove and discard the cinnamon stick.

3 Just before serving, make the sauce. Place the raspberries and fruit cordial in a small pan, bring to a boil, and simmer for 2–3 minutes, until the fruit is just beginning to soften. Stir the marshmallows into the raspberry mixture and heat through, stirring, until the marshmallows begin to melt.

4 Transfer the fruit salad to serving bowls. Top with the raspberry and marshmallow sauce and serve at once.

VARIATION

This sauce is delicious poured over low-fat ice cream. For an extra-colorful sauce, replace the raspberries with an assortment of summer berries.

Citrus Meringue Crush

Serves 4

INGREDIENTS

8 ready-made meringue nests
1¼ cups low-fat natural
    unsweetened yogurt
½ tsp finely grated orange
    rind
½ tsp finely grated lemon rind
½ tsp finely grated lime rind
2 tbsp orange liqueur or
    unsweetened orange juice

TO DECORATE:
sliced kumquat
lime rind, grated

SAUCE:
2 ounces kumquats
8 tbsp unsweetened orange
    juice
2 tbsp lemon juice

2 tbsp lime juice
2 tbsp water
2–3 tsp superfine sugar
1 tsp cornstarch mixed with
    1 tbsp water

1 Place the meringues in a clean plastic bag, seal the bag, and using a rolling pin, crush the meringues into small pieces. Transfer to a mixing bowl.

2 Stir the yogurt, grated citrus rinds, and the liqueur or juice into the crushed meringue. Spoon the mixture into 4 mini-basins, smooth over the tops, and freeze for 1½–2 hours, until firm.

3 To make the sauce, thinly slice the kumquats and place them in a pan with the fruit juices and water. Bring gently to a boil and then simmer over a low heat for 3–4 minutes, until the kumquats have just softened.

4 Sweeten with sugar to taste, stir in the cornstarch mixture, and cook, stirring, until thickened. Pour into a

small bowl, cover the surface with a layer of plastic wrap, and allow to cool—the film will help prevent a skin forming. Chill in the refrigerator.

5 To serve, dip the meringue basins in hot water for 5 seconds, or until they loosen, and turn onto serving plates. Spoon on a little sauce, decorate with slices of kumquat and lime rind, and serve.

Tropical Fruit Fool

Serves 4

INGREDIENTS

1 medium ripe mango
2 kiwi fruit
1 medium banana
2 tbsp lime juice

¹/₂ tsp finely grated lime rind,
    plus extra to decorate
2 medium egg whites
15 ounce can low-fat custard

¹/₂ tsp vanilla extract
2 passion fruit

1 To peel the mango, slice either side of the smooth, flat central pit. Roughly chop the flesh and blend the fruit in a food processor or blender until smooth. Alternatively, mash the chopped mango flesh with a fork.

2 Peel the kiwi fruit, chop the flesh into small pieces, and place in a bowl. Peel and chop the banana and add to the bowl. Toss all of the fruit in the lime juice and rind and mix well to prevent discoloration.

3 In a grease-free bowl, whisk the egg whites until stiff and then gently fold in the custard and vanilla extract until thoroughly mixed.

4 In 4 tall glasses, alternately layer the chopped fruit, mango purée, and custard mixture, finishing with the custard on top. Chill in the refrigerator for 20 minutes.

5 Halve the passion fruits, scoop out the seeds, and spoon the passion fruit over the fruit fools.

6 Decorate each serving with the extra lime rind and serve.

VARIATION

Other tropical fruits to try include papaya purée, with chopped pineapple and dates, and tamarillo or pomegranate seeds to decorate. Or make a summer fruit fool by using strawberry purée, topped with raspberries and blackberries, with cherries to finish.

Brown Sugar Pavlovas

Serves 4

INGREDIENTS

2 large egg whites
1 tsp cornstarch
1 tsp raspberry vinegar
3¹/2 ounces light brown sugar,
    crushed free of lumps
2 tbsp redcurrant jelly

2 tbsp unsweetened orange
    juice
³/4 cup low-fat unsweetened
    yogurt
6 ounces raspberries, thawed
    if frozen

rose-scented geranium leaves,
    to decorate (optional)

1 Preheat the oven to 300°F. Line a large cookie sheet with baking parchment. In a large, grease-free bowl, whisk the egg whites until very stiff and dry. Fold in the cornstarch and vinegar.

2 Gradually whisk in the sugar, a spoonful at a time, until the mixture is thick and glossy.

3 Divide the mixture into 4 and spoon onto the cookie sheet, spaced well apart. Smooth each

into a round, about 4 inches across, and bake in the oven for 40–45 minutes until lightly browned and crisp. Leave to cool on the cookie sheet.

4 Place the redcurrant jelly and orange juice in a small saucepan and heat, stirring, until the jelly has melted. Cool for 10 minutes.

5 Meanwhile, using a spatula, carefully remove each pavlova from the baking parchment and

transfer to a serving plate. Top with unsweetened yogurt and raspberries. Spoon on the redcurrant jelly mixture to glaze. Decorate and serve.

VARIATION

Make a large pavlova by forming the meringue into a round, measuring 7 inches across, on a lined cookie sheet and bake for 1 hour.

Sticky Sesame Bananas

Serves 4

INGREDIENTS

4 ripe medium bananas
3 tbsp lemon juice
4 ounces superfine sugar
4 tbsp cold water

2 tbsp sesame seeds
2/3 cup low-fat unsweetened yogurt
1 tbsp confectioner's sugar
1 tsp vanilla extract

lemon and lime rind, shredded, to decorate

1 Peel the bananas and cut into 2-inch pieces. Place the banana pieces in a bowl, add the lemon juice, and stir well to coat—this will help prevent the bananas from discoloring.

2 Place the sugar and water in a small saucepan and heat gently, stirring, until the sugar dissolves. Bring to a boil and cook for 5–6 minutes, until the mixture turns golden-brown.

3 Meanwhile, drain the bananas and blot with

absorbent paper towels to dry. Line a cookie sheet or board with baking parchment and arrange the bananas, well spaced out, on top.

4 When the caramel is ready, drizzle it over the bananas, working quickly because the caramel sets almost instantly. Sprinkle with the sesame seeds and cool for about 10 minutes.

5 Mix the yogurt with the confectioner's sugar and vanilla extract.

6 Peel the bananas away from the paper and arrange on serving plates. Serve the unsweetened yogurt as a dip, decorated with the shredded lemon and lime rind.

COOK'S TIP

For the best results, use a cannelle knife or a potato peeler to peel away thin strips of rind from the fruit, taking care not to include any bitter pith. Blanch the shreds in boiling water for 1 minute, then refresh in cold water.

Fruit & Fiber Layers

Serves 4

INGREDIENTS

4 ounces dried apricots
4 ounces dried prunes
4 ounces dried peaches
2 ounces dried apple
1 ounce dried cherries

2 cups unsweetened apple
 juice
6 cardamom pods
6 cloves
1 cinnamon stick, broken

1 1/4 cups low-fat
 unsweetened yogurt
14 ounces crunchy oat cereal

TO DECORATE:
apricot slices

1 To make the fruit compote, place the dried apricots, prunes, peaches, apples, and cherries in a saucepan and pour in the apple juice.

2 Add the cardamom pods, cloves, and cinnamon stick to the pan, bring to a boil, and simmer for 10–15 minutes, until the fruits are plump and tender.

3 Allow the mixture to cool completely in the pan, then transfer the mixture to a bowl, and leave to chill in the refrigerator for 1 hour. Remove and discard the spices from the fruits.

4 Spoon the compote into 4 dessert glasses, layering it alternately with yogurt and oat cereal, finishing with the oat cereal on top.

5 Decorate each dessert with slices of apricot and serve at once.

COOK'S TIP

There are many dried fruits available, including mangoes and pears, some of which need soaking, so read the instructions on the packet before use. Also, check the ingredients label, because several types of dried fruit have added sugar or are rolled in sugar, and this will affect the sweetness of the dish that you use them in.

Pan-Cooked Apples in Red Wine

Serves 4

INGREDIENTS

4 eating apples
2 tbsp lemon juice
1 1/2 ounces low-fat spread
2 ounces light brown sugar
1 small orange

1 cinnamon stick, broken
2/3 cup red wine
8 ounces raspberries, hulled
    and thawed if frozen

sprigs of fresh mint, to
    decorate

1 Peel and core the apples, then cut them into thick wedges. Place the apples in a bowl and toss in the lemon juice to prevent the fruit from discoloring.

2 In a skillet, gently melt the low-fat spread over a low heat, add the sugar, and stir to form a paste.

3 Stir the apple wedges into the skillet and cook, stirring occasionally, for 2 minutes, or until the apples are coated in the sugar paste.

4 Using a vegetable peeler, pare off a few strips of orange rind. Add the orange rind to the pan, along with the cinnamon pieces. Extract the juice from the orange and pour into the pan with the red wine. Bring to a boil, then simmer for 10 minutes, stirring.

5 Add the raspberries to the pan and cook for 5 minutes, or until the apples are tender.

6 Discard the orange rind and cinnamon

pieces. Transfer the apple and raspberry mixture to a serving plate, together with the wine sauce. Decorate with a sprig of fresh mint and serve hot.

VARIATION

For other fruity combinations, cook the apples with blackberries, blackcurrants, or redcurrants. You may need to add more sugar if you use currants, as they are not as sweet as raspberries.

Broiled Fruit Platter with Lime Butter

Serves 4

INGREDIENTS

1 baby pineapple	4 tbsp dark rum	LIME BUTTER:
1 ripe papaya	1 tsp ground allspice	2 ounces low-fat spread
1 ripe mango	2 tbsp lime juice	1/2 tsp finely grated lime rind
2 kiwi fruit	4 tbsp dark brown sugar	1 tbsp confectioner's sugar
4 finger bananas		

1 Quarter the pineapple, trimming away most of the leaves, and place in a shallow dish. Peel the papaya, cut it in half, and scoop out the seeds. Cut the flesh into thick wedges and place in the same dish as the pineapple.

2 Peel the mango, cut either side of the smooth, central flat pit and remove the pit. Slice the flesh into thick wedges. Peel the kiwi fruit and cut in half. Peel the bananas. Add all of these fruits to the dish.

3 Sprinkle with the rum, allspice, and lime juice, cover, and leave at room temperature for about 30 minutes, turning occasionally, to allow the flavors to develop.

4 Meanwhile, make the lime butter. Place the low-fat spread in a small bowl and beat in the lime rind and sugar until well mixed. Chill until the butter is required.

5 Preheat the broiler. Drain the fruit, reserving the juices, and arrange in the broiler pan. Sprinkle with the sugar and broil for 3–4 minutes until hot and just beginning to char.

6 Transfer the fruit to a serving plate and spoon the juices on top. Serve the fruit with the lime butter.

VARIATION

Serve with a light sauce of 1 1/4 cups tropical fruit juice thickened with 2 tsp arrowroot.

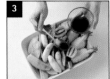

Baked Pears with Cinnamon & Brown Sugar

Serves 4

INGREDIENTS

4 ripe pears	1 tsp ground cinnamon	lemon rind, finely grated, to
2 tbsp lemon juice	2 ounces low-fat spread	decorate
4 tbsp light brown sugar	low-fat custard, to serve	

1 Preheat the oven to 400°F. Core and peel the pears, then slice them in half lengthwise, and brush all over with the lemon juice to prevent the pears from discoloring. Place the pears, cored side down, in a small nonstick roasting pan.

2 Place the sugar, cinnamon, and low-fat spread in a small saucepan and heat gently, stirring, until the sugar has melted. Keep the heat low to stop too much water evaporating from the low-fat spread as it gets hot. Spoon the mixture over the pears.

3 Bake in the oven for 20–25 minutes, or until the pears are tender and golden, occasionally spooning the sugar mixture over the fruit during the cooking time.

4 To serve, heat the custard until it is piping hot and spoon over the bases of 4 warm dessert plates. Arrange 2 pear halves on each plate. Decorate and serve.

VARIATION

This recipe also works well if you use cooking apples. For alternative flavors, replace the cinnamon with ground ginger, and serve the pears sprinkled with chopped, preserved ginger in syrup. Alternatively, use ground allspice and spoon warm dark rum on top.

Baked Apples with Blackberries

Serves 4

INGREDIENTS

4 medium-size cooking apples
1 tbsp lemon juice
3 1/2 ounces prepared
   blackberries, thawed if
   frozen
1/2 ounce slivered almonds
1/2 tsp ground allspice

1/2 tsp finely grated lemon
   rind
2 tbsp raw crystal sugar
1 1/4 cups ruby port
1 cinnamon stick, broken
2 tsp cornstarch blended with
   2 tbsp cold water

low-fat custard, to serve

1 Preheat the oven to 400°F. Wash and dry the apples. Using a small sharp knife, make a shallow cut through the skin around the middle of each apple—this will help the apples to cook through.

2 Core the apples, brush the centers with the lemon juice to prevent browning, and stand in a shallow ovenproof dish.

3 In a bowl, mix together the

blackberries, almonds, allspice, lemon rind, and sugar. Using a teaspoon, spoon the mixture into the center of each apple.

4 Pour the port into the dish, add the cinnamon stick, and bake the apples in the oven for 35–40 minutes, or until tender. Drain the cooking juices into a pan and keep the apples warm.

5 Discard the cinnamon and add the cornstarch mixture to the cooking

juices. Heat, stirring, until thickened.

6 Heat the custard until piping hot. Pour the sauce over the apples and serve with the custard.

VARIATION

Use raspberries instead of blackberries and, if you prefer, replace the port with unsweetened orange juice.

Fruity Skewers with Chocolate Dipping Sauce

Serves 4

INGREDIENTS

selection of fruit (choose from oranges, bananas, strawberries, pineapple chunks (fresh or canned), apricots (fresh or canned), eating apples, pears, kiwi fruit)	1 tbsp lemon juice CHOCOLATE SAUCE: 4 tbsp butter 4 squares dark chocolate, broken into small cubes 1/2 tbsp cocoa powder	2 tbsp corn syrup BASTE: 4 tbsp clear honey grated rind and juice of 1/2 orange

1 To make the chocolate sauce, place the butter, chocolate, cocoa powder, and corn syrup in a small pan. Heat gently at the side of the barbecue, stirring continuously, until all of the ingredients have melted and are well combined.

2 To prepare the fruit, peel and core if necessary, then cut into large, bite-size pieces or wedges as appropriate. Dip apples, pears, and bananas in lemon juice to prevent discoloration. Thread the pieces of fruit onto skewers.

3 To make the baste, mix together the honey, orange juice and rind, heat gently if required, and brush over the fruit.

4 Broil the fruit skewers over warm coals for 5–10 minutes, until hot. Serve with the chocolate dipping sauce.

COOK'S TIP

If the coals are too hot, raise the rack so that it is about 6 inches above the coals or spread out the coals a little to reduce the heat. Do not assemble the fruit skewers more than 1–2 hours before they are required.

Toffee Fruit Kabobs

Serves 4

INGREDIENTS

2 eating apples, cored and cut into wedges	2 tbsp light brown sugar	SAUCE:
2 firm pears, cored and cut into wedges	$1/4$ tsp ground allspice	9 tbsp butter
juice of $1/2$ lemon	2 tbsp unsalted butter, melted	$1/2$ cup light brown sugar
		6 tbsp heavy cream

1 Toss the apple and pears in the lemon juice to prevent any discoloration.

2 Mix the sugar and allspice together and sprinkle over the fruit.

3 Carefully thread the fruit pieces onto skewers.

4 To make the toffee sauce, place the butter and sugar in a saucepan and heat, stirring gently, until the butter has melted and the sugar has dissolved.

5 Add the cream to the saucepan and bring to a boil. Boil for 1–2 minutes, then set aside to cool slightly.

6 Meanwhile, place the fruit kabobs over hot coals and broil for about 5 minutes, turning and basting frequently with the melted butter, until the fruit is just tender.

7 Transfer the fruit kabobs to warm serving plates and serve with the slightly cooled toffee sauce.

COOK'S TIP

Firm apples that will keep their shape are needed for this dish—varieties such as Golden Delicious, Granny Smith and Braeburn are a good choice. Soft apples and pears will become mushy as they cook.

VARIATION

Sprinkle the fruit kabobs with chopped walnuts or pecans before serving, if you wish.

Baked Bananas

Serves 4

INGREDIENTS

4 bananas	ORANGE-FLAVORED CREAM:
2 passion fruit	2/3 cup heavy cream
4 tbsp orange juice	3 tbsp confectioners' sugar
4 tbsp orange-flavored liqueur	2 tbsp orange-flavored liqueur

1 Peel the bananas and place each one onto a sheet of foil.

2 Cut the passion fruit in half and squeeze the juice of each half over each banana. Spoon the orange juice and liqueur over each banana.

3 Fold the kitchen foil over the top of the bananas to enclose them.

4 Cook the bananas over hot coals for about 10 minutes, or until they are warm and just tender.

5 To make the orange-flavored cream, pour the heavy cream into a mixing bowl and sprinkle with the confectioners' sugar. Whisk the mixture until it is standing in soft peaks. Carefully fold in the orange-flavored liqueur and chill in the refrigerator until required.

6 Transfer the foil packets containing the bananas to warm, individual serving plates. Open the foil packets at the table and then serve the bananas immediately together with the orange-flavored cream.

VARIATION

Leave the bananas in their skins for a really quick dessert. Split the banana skins and put in 1–2 squares of chocolate. Wrap the bananas in foil and barbecue for 10 minutes, or until the chocolate just melts.

Rocky Road Bites

Makes 18

INGREDIENTS

4¹/₂ ounces milk chocolate
2¹/₂ ounces mini multicolored
 marshmallows

¹/₄ cup chopped walnuts
1 ounce no-need-to-soak dried
 apricots, chopped

1 Line a cookie sheet with baking parchment and set aside.

2 Break the milk chocolate into small pieces and melt in a double boiler.

3 Stir in the marsh-mallows, walnuts, and apricots and toss in the melted chocolate until the ingredients are completely coated in the chocolate.

4 Place heaping teaspoons of the mixture onto the prepared cookie sheet.

5 Chill the candies in the refrigerator until they are completely set.

6 Once set, carefully remove the candies from the baking parchment.

7 The chewy bites can be placed in paper candy cases to serve, if desired.

COOK'S TIP

These candies can be stored in a cool, dry place for up to 2 weeks.

VARIATION

Light, fluffy marshmallows are available in white or pastel colors. If you cannot find mini marshmallows, use large ones and snip them into smaller pieces with kitchen scissors before mixing them into the melted chocolate in step 3.

Easy Chocolate Fudge

Makes 25-30 pieces

INGREDIENTS

1 lb 2 ounces dark chocolate
⅓ cup sweet butter

14 ounce can sweetened condensed milk

½ tsp vanilla extract

1 Lightly grease an 8-inch square cake pan.

2 Break the chocolate into pieces and place in a large saucepan with the butter and condensed milk.

3 Heat gently, stirring until the chocolate and butter melt and the mixture is smooth. Do not allow to boil.

4 Remove the pan from the heat. Beat in the vanilla extract, then beat the mixture for a few minutes until thickened. Pour it into the prepared pan and level the top.

5 Chill the mixture in the refrigerator until firm.

6 Tip the fudge out onto a cutting board and cut into squares to serve.

VARIATION

For chocolate peanut fudge, replace 4 tablespoons of the butter with crunchy peanut butter.

COOK'S TIP

Store the fudge in an airtight container in a cool, dry place for up to 1 month. Do not freeze.

COOK'S TIP

Don't use milk chocolate as the results will be too sticky.

No-Cook Fruit & Nut Chocolate Fudge

Makes about 25 pieces

INGREDIENTS

9 ounces dark chocolate	4 tbsp evaporated milk	1/2 cup roughly chopped hazelnuts
2 tbsp butter	3 cups confectioners' sugar, sifted	1/3 cup golden raisins

1 Lightly grease an 8-inch square cake pan.

2 Break the chocolate into pieces and melt in a double boiler with the butter and evaporated milk. Stir until the chocolate and butter have melted and the ingredients are well combined.

3 Remove from the heat and gradually beat in the confectioners' sugar. Stir the hazelnuts and golden raisins into the mixture. Press the fudge into the prepared pan and level the top. Chill until the fudge is firm.

4 Tip the fudge out onto a cutting board and cut into squares. Place in paper candy cases. Chill until required.

VARIATION

Vary the nuts used in this recipe; try making the fudge with almonds, brazil nuts, walnuts, or pecans.

COOK'S TIP

The fudge can be stored in an airtight container for up to 2 weeks.

Nutty Chocolate Clusters

Makes about 30

INGREDIENTS

6 ounces white chocolate
3 1/2 ounces graham crackers

1 cup chopped macadamia nuts or
brazil nuts

1 ounce preserved ginger,
chopped (optional)
6 ounces dark chocolate

1 Line a cookie sheet with baking parchment. Break the white chocolate into small pieces and melt in a double boiler.

2 Break the graham crackers into small pieces. Stir the graham crackers into the melted chocolate, together with the chopped nuts and preserved ginger, if using.

3 Place heaping teaspoons of the mixture onto the prepared cookie sheet.

4 Chill the mixture in the refrigerator until set, then carefully remove the clusters from the baking parchment.

5 Melt the dark chocolate and let cool slightly. Dip the clusters into the melted chocolate, allowing the excess to drip back into the bowl. Return the clusters to the cookie sheet and chill in the refrigerator until set.

COOK'S TIP

The clusters can be stored for up to 1 week in a cool, dry place.

COOK'S TIP

Macadamia and brazil nuts are both rich-tasting and high in fat, which makes them particularly popular for confectionery, but other nuts can be used, if desired.

Chocolate Cherries

Makes 24

INGREDIENTS

12 candied cherries	9 ounces marzipan	extra milk, dark, or white chocolate,
2 tbsp rum or brandy	5½ ounces dark chocolate	to decorate (optional)

1 Line a cookie sheet with baking parchment.

2 Cut the cherries in half and place them in a small bowl. Add the rum or brandy and stir to coat. Set the cherries aside to soak for a minimum of 1 hour, stirring occasionally.

3 Divide the marzipan into 24 pieces and roll each piece into a ball. Press half a marinated cherry into the top of each marzipan ball.

4 Break the chocolate into pieces and melt in a double boiler.

5 Dip each candy into the melted chocolate, allowing the excess to drip back into the pan. Place the coated cherries on the baking parchment and chill until set.

6 If desired, melt a little extra chocolate and drizzle it over the top of the coated cherries. Let set.

VARIATION

Flatten the marzipan and use it to mold around the cherries to cover them, then dip in the chocolate as above.

VARIATION

Use a whole almond in place of the halved candied cherries and omit the rum or brandy.

Chocolate Marzipans

Makes about 30

INGREDIENTS

1 pound marzipan	1 ounce preserved ginger, very	12 ounces dark chocolate
1/3 cup very finely chopped	finely chopped	1 ounces white chocolate
candied cherries	1/4 cup no-need-to-soak dried	confectioners' sugar, to dust
	apricots, very finely chopped	

1 Line a cookie sheet with baking parchment. Divide the marzipan into 3 balls and knead each ball to soften it.

2 Work the candied cherries into one portion of the marzipan by kneading on a surface lightly dusted with confectioners' sugar.

3 Work the preserved ginger into a second portion of marzipan, and then work the apricots into the third portion of marzipan in the same way.

4 Form each flavored portion of marzipan into small balls, making sure the flavors are kept separate.

5 Melt the dark chocolate in a double boiler. Dip one of each flavored ball of marzipan into the chocolate by spiking each one with a toothpick, allowing the excess chocolate to drip back into the pan.

6 Carefully place the balls in clusters of the three flavors on the prepared cookie sheet. Repeat with the remaining marzipan balls. Chill until set.

7 Melt the white chocolate and drizzle a little over the tops of each cluster of marzipan balls. Chill until hardened, then remove from the baking parchment and dust with sugar to serve.

VARIATION

Coat the marzipan balls in white or milk chocolate and drizzle with dark chocolate, if desired.